GUIDE TO PRIMARY WESTERN-LANGUAGE
SOURCES FOR ASIAN STUDIES
IN THE STANFORD UNIVERSITY LIBRARIES

compiled under the direction of

Ramon H. Myers

East Asian Collection
Hoover Institution on War, Revolution and Peace

Hoover Institution   Stanford University

GUIDE TO PRIMARY WESTERN-LANGUAGE
SOURCES FOR ASIAN STUDIES
IN THE STANFORD UNIVERSITY LIBRARIES

GUIDE TO PRIMARY WESTERN-LANGUAGE
SOURCES FOR ASIAN STUDIES
IN THE STANFORD UNIVERSITY LIBRARIES

compiled under the direction of

Ramon H. Myers

East Asian Collection
Hoover Institution on War, Revolution and Peace

Hoover Institution   Stanford University

The Hoover Institution on War, Revolution and Peace, founded at Stanford University in 1919 by the late President Herbert Hoover, is an interdisciplinary research center for advanced study on domestic and international affairs in the twentieth century. The views expressed in its publications are entirely those of the authors and do not necessarily reflect the views of the staff, officers, or Board of Overseers of the Hoover Institution.

Hoover Press Bibliography 69

© 1986 by the Board of Trustees of the Leland Stanford Junior University

All rights reserved. No part of this publication may be reproduced, stored in a retrieval system, or transmitted in any form or by any means, electronic, mechanical, photocopying, recording, or otherwise, without written permission of the publisher.

First printing, 1986

Manufactured in the United States of America

90 89 88 87 86   9 8 7 6 5 4 3 2 1

Library of Congress Cataloging-in-Publication Data

Hoover Institution on War, Revolution and Peace. East Asian Collection.
  Guide to primary Western-language sources for Asian studies in the Stanford University Libraries / compiled under the direction of Ramon H. Myers.

  (Hoover Press bibliographical series ; 69)

  1. East Asia--Bibliography--Catalogs. 2. Stanford University. Libraries--Catalogs. I. Myers, Ramon Hawley, 1929- . II. Title. III. Series.
Z3001.H66 1986 [DS504.5]   016.95   86-20166
ISBN 0-8179-2692-5

CONTENTS

Primary Subject	Subsection Prefix	Page
CHINA		
Chinese Customs Publications	1	3
Miscellaneous Chinese Govt. Sources	2	6
British Consular Service Records	3	9
British Colonial/Foreign Office Material	4	9
Miscellaneous British Govt. Sources	5	14
U.S. Diplomatic Records	6	15
U.S. Central Intelligence Agency Material	7	18
U.S. State Dept. Material	8	19
Miscellaneous U.S. Govt. Sources	9	22
Miscellaneous Sources	10	23
JAPAN		
Japanese Govt. Sources on Foreign Relations	11	31
Japanese Govt. Sources on Economic Conditions	12	32
Miscellaneous Japanese Govt. Sources	13	35
British Foreign Office Material	14	37
Miscellaneous British Govt. Sources	15	39
U.S. Diplomatic Records	16	39
U.S. State Dept. Material	17	41
U.S. Govt. Sources: World War II	18	43
U.S. Govt. Sources: Internment of Japanese-Americans During World War II	19	47
U.S. Govt. Sources: Postwar Japan	20	48
Miscellaneous U.S. Govt. Sources	21	50
Miscellaneous Sources	22	51
MANCHURIA		
Manchurian Govt. Publications	23	61
Japanese Sources	24	62
British and U.S. Govt. Sources	25	64
Miscellaneous Sources	26	64
KOREA		
Korean Govt. Sources	27	69
U.S. Govt. Sources on Relations with Korea	28	70
Miscellaneous U.S. Govt. Sources	29	71
Korean War: Origins and Settlement	30	72
Korean War: Military Operations	31	75
Korean War: Prisoners of War	32	76
Miscellaneous Sources	33	77
MISCELLANEOUS		
Southeast Asia and the Vietnam War	34	83
The Far East in General	35	85
INDEX	--	87

INTRODUCTION

This volume comprises a selection of source materials, primarily large compilations, chosen from the card catalogs of the Green Library and Hoover Institution of Stanford University. The bulk of these primary materials are ultimately the work of official bodies or serve to reflect their views.

Material from the Hoover Archives has been excluded, as have been most serials, guidebooks, personal and travel accounts, bibliographies, and directories. Obvious propaganda and most recently published material have also been excluded. It is felt that most of the foregoing exclusions are likely to be either too topical or too desultory for a work of this scope; all, too, should be readily accessible through the appropriate card catalogs.

The listings themselves are modified transcriptions of selected records from the card catalogs, and reflect Stanford's holdings as of June 1986.

Arrangements under the major headings (China, Japan, etc.) vary substantially, in line with the differing natures of the available source materials. In all cases, however, the material in each (separately prefixed) subsection appears in approximate order of its chronological coverage.

Holdings of multivolume works have generally been fully noted. In a few instances, however, in which complete holdings were not readily available, or in which a full listing would have been unprofitably cumbersome, the notation [ ] has been used. Thus, "[no.1-101, 1958-67//]" indicates that the library owns no.1 (1958) and no.101 (1967), as well as scattered holdings in between. In most cases it may be safely assumed that the library owns most of the intervening material. (The notation "//" in the above example indicates that no.101 (1967) was the last issue published.)

Where no holdings are indicated for a multivolume work, the library owns the complete set.

Works held in more than one location are generally listed for only one location, with Green Library copies being preferred, as most of the sources listed are housed there. Location abbreviations and their equivalents are as follows:

GOV	Jonsson Library of Government Documents, Green Lib.
GOV REF	Reference section, Jonsson Library of Government Documents, Green Lib.
GSB	Jackson Library, Graduate School of Business
HOV	Hoover Institution stacks
HOV (EAC)	East Asian Collection Reading Room, Hoover Institution
Mss Dept.	Manuscripts Dept., Special Collection, Green Lib.
MTXT	Current Periodicals/Microtext Div., Green Lib.
STK	Green Library stacks
STK/CPR	Current issues in Current Periodicals/Microtext Div., Green Lib.; back issues in Green Lib. stacks
STK/GOV	Current issues in Jonsson Library of Government Documents, Green Lib.; back issues in Green Lib. stacks

The final section of this volume is a combined index to all sections of the bibliography, with entries transcribed from the card catalogs. Series access points, however, have been neither noted nor traced. Index entries have, as a rule, been transcribed directly from the catalog tracings. In cases where the precision or the generality of an entry seemed disproportionate to the scope of this work, however, the catalog entry was either omitted or modified. It is advisable to try all reasonable subject-entry possibilities, with special regard to their subdivisions.

Filing of index entries follows the practice of the Green Library catalog. The one prominent deviation is that filing is letter-by-letter, not word-by-word. Thus, e.g., "economical annual" precedes "economic annual."

Except where noted, upper-case entries are subject entries. In line with Green Library filing practice, chronological subdivisions of subject entries precede all other subdivisions.

Most punctuation is ignored in filing, with two prominent exceptions: The semicolon between title and subtitle is considered a "stop" delimiting two filing elements, as is also the comma between a surname and a given name. The break between author and title is, of course, also considered a "stop."

With these provisos, filing is strictly alphabetical. (In accordance with common practice, a surname beginning with "Mc-" is filed as though it began with "Mac-"; acronyms generally file before words; and "U.S." is filed as though spelled out, "United States.")

When conflicts between identical filing elements occur, they are resolved as follows: An author entry precedes a subject entry, which in turn precedes a title entry.

Index references are to the decimal numbers at the beginning of each listing in the bibliography section. Each number is filed as a single element; thus, 14.102 precedes 14.12.

Source Materials on China

CHINESE CUSTOMS PUBLICATIONS

1.1   China. Hai kuan tsung shui wu ssu shu.
      Reports on trade at the treaty ports. [1st]-17th issue; 1865-81. Shanghai, 1866-82.

   Title varies: 1865-66, Reports on the trade at the ports in China open by treaty to foreign trade; 1867-76, Reports on trade at the treaty ports in China.
   Continued as part of its Returns of trade and trade reports.

      LIBRARY HAS: 1-17 (1865-81)//
      MFILM N.S. 1744 MTXT

1.11 Returns of trade at the treaty ports in China.   Shanghai.

      LIBRARY HAS: [1868-69]
      HF3831.R45 STK

1.112 Imperial Maritime Customs. III, Miscellaneous series.
      Shanghai : published by order of the Inspector General of Chinese Maritime Customs.

      LIBRARY HAS: 3, 5, 9-14, 29, 48-49
      MFILM N.S. 7548 MTXT

1.114 China. Hai kuan tsung shui wu ssu shu.
      Service list. Shanghai : Statistical Dept. of the Inspectorate General of Customs.

   Other title: Hsin kuan ti ming lu.

      LIBRARY HAS: 1-8, 1874-81; 10-14, 1884-88; 21-39, 1895-1913
      MFILM N.S. 7519 MTXT

1.116 Imperial Maritime Customs. V, Office series. Customs papers.
      Shanghai : Statistical Dept. of the Inspectorate General.

      LIBRARY HAS: 4, 12, 27, 71, 85, 88
      MFILM N.S. 7549 MTXT

1.118   Returns of trade at the treaty ports. 1881-86.
        Shanghai : Statistical Dept. of the Inspectorate General,
        1881-86.

           Other title: Returns of trade at the treaty
        ports, and trade reports.
           Continued by returns of trade and trade reports.

              LIBRARY HAS: 1881-86//
              MFILM N.S. 7522 MTXT

1.119   Imperial Maritime Customs. I, Special series. no. 2- .
        Shanghai : published by order of the Inspector General
        of Customs, 1881- .

           No. 1 never published?

              LIBRARY HAS: 4-11, 13, 17, 27, 29, 31
              MFILM N.S. 7521 MTXT

1.12   China. Hai kuan tsung shui wu ssu shu.
           Decennial reports on the trade, navigation, industries, etc.
        of the ports open to foreign commerce in China and Corea...

              LIBRARY HAS: 1st-2d issues (1882/91-1892/1901)
              MFILM N.S. 7567 MTXT

              LIBRARY HAS: 3d issue (1902-11), v.1-3; 4th issue
                 (1912-21), v.1-2; 5th issue (1922-31), v.1-2
              382.51.C539d STK

1.13   China. Hai kuan tsung shui wu ssu shu.
           Medical reports. no. 1-80. Shanghai, 1871-1910.

              LIBRARY HAS: no.14-16, 33-50, 58, 60-64 (1903-10)
              614.0951.C574 STK

1.14   China. Hai kuan tsung shui wu ssu shu.
           Quarterly returns of trade.

           Title varies: 1909-13, Customs gazette.

              LIBRARY HAS: no.1-8, 11-12, 29-30, 36, 161-204 (1909-19)
              382.51.C539c STK

1.16   China. Hai kuan tsung shui wu ssu shu.
            Returns of trade and trade reports. 1887-1919.
        Shanghai.

            Continues Returns of trade at the treaty ports.
            Continued by its Foreign trade of China.

                LIBRARY HAS: 1904:1; 1907:1b; 1908-19//; Index, 1913-17
                382.51.C539r   STK

                LIBRARY HAS: 1887-1909; 1914; 1918-19//
                MFILM N.S. 7522   MTXT

1.18   China. Hai kuan tsung shui wu ssu shu.
            Foreign trade of China. 1920-31. Shanghai, 1921-32.

            Continues parts 1 and 3 of its Returns of trade and trade
        reports.
            Continued by its Trade of China.

                LIBRARY HAS: 1920-31//
                382.51.C539r   STK

1.2   China. Hai kuan tsung shui wu ssu shu.
            Annual trade report and returns. 1920-   . Shanghai,
        1921-   .

                LIBRARY HAS: 1920-31
                382.51.C539a   STK

1.22   China. Hai kuan tsung shui wu ssu shu.
            Monthly returns of the foreign trade of China. Nov. 1931-   .
        [Shanghai].

            Publication suspended May 1943?-June 1946.
            Some issues accompanied by supplements and appendices.
            Absorbed its Shanghai monthly returns of trade, Jan. 1947.

                LIBRARY HAS: 1932; Dec. 1934; Dec. 1935; Dec. 1936;
                   Jan-Dec. 1937; June, Aug. 1939; 1944; Jan-Aug. 1945;
                   July, Oct., Dec. 1946; 1947-48
                HF237.A44   STK

                LIBRARY HAS: 1936-38; July-Dec. 1946; 1947; Jan-May 1948
                MFILM N.S. 7520   MTXT

1.24   China. Hai kuan tsung shui wu ssu shu.
       The trade of China. 1932- . Shanghai, 1933- .

      Continues its Foreign trade of China and its Returns of trade and trade reports.

        LIBRARY HAS: 1932-43; 1946:1-3; 1947:2-4; 1948:3;
          1950-78; 1980-
        382.51.C539r STK

        LIBRARY HAS: 1935-48
        MFILM N.S. 7523 MTXT

1.26   China. Hai kuan tsung shui wu ssu shu.
      Trade statistics of the treaty ports, for the period 1863-1872. Compiled for the Austro-Hungarian Universal Exhibition, Vienna, 1873... Shanghai, 1873.

        HF3771.A4 1873 STK

1.28   China. Treaties, etc.
      Treaties, conventions, etc. between China and foreign states. 2d ed. Shanghai : Inspectorate General of Customs, 1917.

      Partial contents: II. Belgium, Sweden and Norway, Sweden, Germany, Portugal, Denmark, The Netherlands, Spain, Italy, Austria-Hungary, Japan, Peru, Brazil, Congo Free State, Mexico, Korea.

        341.251.C539 1917 STK

1.3   China. Hai kuan tsung shui wu ssu shu.
      The collection and disposal of the maritime and native customs revenue since the revolution of 1911. ed. 2. Shanghai : Inspectorate General of Customs, 1927.

        336.51.C539 STK

MISCELLANEOUS CHINESE GOVERNMENT SOURCES

2.1   China. Legation (U.S.)
     Notes from the Chinese Legation in the United States to the Department of State, 1868-1906. Washington : National Archives, 1947.
     6 reels.

        MFILM N.S. 711 MTXT

2.12   China.
    The Chino-Japanese negotiations. Chinese official statement with documents and treaties with annexures.   Peking, 1915.

    327.51.C539   STK

2.14   China. Wai chiao pu.
    Official documents relating to the war. (For the year 1917). [Peking : Printed by the "Peking leader" press, 1918].

    D505.C539   HOV

2.16   The Chinese economic bulletin. v. 1-27; Jan. 25, 1921-Dec. 28, 1935.   Shanghai, 1927-35.

    Issued by the Bureau of Economic Information, Peking, 1921- ; by the Bureau of Industrial and Economic Information,   -June 1931; by the Bureau of Foreign Trade, July 1931-1935.
    Title varies: 1921-Sept. 8, 1923, Bulletin prepared for circulation abroad.
    Merged with Chinese economic journal to form Chinese economic journal and bulletin.

    LIBRARY HAS: [1921-26]; 1927-28; [1929-35]//
    330.5.C537   STK

2.18   China. National Tariff Commission.
    The Shanghai market prices report.   Jan/Mar. 1923-[Oct/Dec. 1933].   Shanghai, [1923-34?].

    Issued by the Bureau of Markets, 1923-28.
    Continued by its Annual report of Shanghai commodity prices.

    LIBRARY HAS: Apr/June 1923-Oct/Dec. 1933//
    338.50951.C539   STK

2.2   The Chinese economic monthly. v. 1-3; Oct. 1923-Dec. 1926.   Peking : Chinese Government Bureau of Economic Information, 1923-26.

    Superseded by: Chinese economic journal [and bulletin].

    LIBRARY HAS: v. 1-3, 1923-26//
      WANTING v. 1, no. 1
    330.5.C538   STK

2.22　Chinese economic journal and bulletin. v. 1-20; Jan. 1927-June 1937. [Shanghai] : Bureau of Foreign Trade, Ministry of Industry [etc., 1927-37].

　　　Supersedes Chinese economic monthly.
　　　Title varies: 1927-35, Chinese economic journal.

　　　　　LIBRARY HAS: v. 1-20, 1927-37//
　　　　　　WANTING v. 4, no. 5
　　　　　330.5.C539　STK

2.24　China. National Tariff Commission.
　　　Prices and price indexes in Shanghai.　Shanghai.

　　　　　LIBRARY HAS: no. 5-9, 13, 15 (1929-38)
　　　　　338.50951.C539p

2.26　China. Ministry of Finance.
　　　Annual report. 1911/12-　. Nanking, 1912-　.

　　　　　LIBRARY HAS: 1928/29-1934/35
　　　　　336.51.C538

2.28　The Statistical monthly. no. 1-　; March 1929-　.
　　　Nanking, 1929-　.

　　　1929-32 published by the Bureau of Statistics, Legislative Yuan; 1933-　by the Directorate of Statistics, Directorate-General of Budgets, Accounts and Statistics.
　　　Title varies: Mar. 1929-Dec. 1934, no. 1-26, Statistical monthly; Mar. 1935-Dec. 1936, no. 1-8, Quarterly journal of statistics.

　　　　　LIBRARY HAS: no. 9-30, Jan. 1933-July 1937
　　　　　315.1.S797　STK

2.3　China. Ministry of Foreign Affairs.
　　　Information bulletin. no. 1-　; Apr. 10, 1933-　.
　　　Nanking, [1933-　].

　　　　　LIBRARY HAS: no. 1-8, Apr. 10-July 25, 1933
　　　　　DS701.A2　HOV

2.32　China. National Tariff Commission.
　　　An annual report of Shanghai commodity prices, 1934-　.
　　　[China], 1934-　.

　　　　　LIBRARY HAS: 1937
　　　　　338.50951.C539a　STK

BRITISH CONSULAR SERVICE RECORDS

3.1   Great Britain. Consulate, Peking.
      Despatches from Sir A. Hosie, forwarding reports respecting the opium question in China.   London : HMSO, [1911].

        Brit.Doc. C1911 v.103 GOV

3.12   Great Britain. Consulate, Peking.
      Reports from His Majesty's minister at Peking respecting the opium question in China.   London : HMSO, 1913.

        Brit.Doc. C1913 v.81 GOV

3.14   Great Britain. Consulate, Tamsui, Formosa.
      Report by Mr. Hosie on the Island of Formosa, with special reference to its resources and trade.   London : HMSO, [1893].

        Brit.Doc. C1893 v.89 GOV

BRITISH COLONIAL/FOREIGN OFFICE MATERIAL

4.1   Great Britain. Public Record Office.
      General correspondence: China, 1815-1905.   [London, 1970-76].
      1045 reels.

        MFILM N.S. 728 MTXT

4.102   Great Britain. Public Record Office.
      Registers and indexes of general correspondence: China, 1815-1890.   [London, 1974].
      9 reels.

        MFILM N.S. 1229 MTXT

4.104   Great Britain. Public Record Office.
      Registers of general correspondence: China, Japan, Siam, Korea, 1891-1919.   [London, 1974].
      19 reels.

        LIBRARY LACKS: Reel 3:24842
        MFILM N.S. 1228 MTXT

4.12   Great Britain. Foreign Office.
   Embassy and consular archives: China correspondence, 1834-1894.   [London] : Public Record Office, 1970-[76?]. 575 reels.

   MFILM N.S. 729   MTXT

4.14   Great Britain. Foreign Office.
   Foreign Office confidential papers relating to China and her neighbouring countries, 1840-1914; with an Additional list 1915-1937 / [compiled by] Lo Hui-min.   The Hague and Paris : Mouton, 1969.

   CD1051.A42   GOV

4.16   Great Britain. Treaties, etc.
   List of treaties, etc. between Great Britain and China (1842-1922), including international treaties, and treaties between Great Britain and foreign powers relating to China. London : HMSO, 1925.

   341.242.G786c   STK
   Another copy: Brit.Doc. 1924-25 v.30   GOV

4.18   Great Britain. Public Record Office.
   Confidential print: China, 1848-1922.   [London, 1970]. 32 reels.

   MFILM N.S. 727   MTXT
   Mfilm ed. of 1923-37 on order for MTXT

4.182   Great Britain. Public Record Office.
   A guide to British Foreign Office: Confidential print: China, 1848-1922 (Microfilm F.O. 405) / by Carol Reynolds.   New York : Columbia University, East Asian Institute, 1970.

   Z3106.G7   GOV

4.2   Great Britain. Foreign Office. 1871.
   Papers relating to the massacre of Europeans at Tien-Tsin, 21st June, 1870.   London : Harrison & Sons, [1871].

   Brit.Doc. C1871 v.70   GOV

4.22   Great Britain. Foreign Office. 1878.
       Report by Mr. Baber on the route followed by Mr. Grosvenor's mission between Tali-fu and Momein.   London : Harrison & Sons, [1878].

       Brit.Doc. C1878 v.75   GOV

4.24   Great Britain. Foreign Office.
       [Embassy and consular archives, China, Shanghai supreme court, various cases, 1884-1891].   [London] : Public Record Office, [1975].
       2 reels.

       MFILM N.S. 1575   MTXT

4.26   Great Britain. Foreign Office.
       Reports from Her Majesty's minister in China respecting events at Peking...December 1900.   London : HMSO, c[1900?].

       DS770.G74 1900   STK

4.28   Great Britain. Foreign Office.
       Correspondence respecting the disturbances in China.
       London : HMSO, 1901.

       DS740.6.G5A29   HOV (Sokolsky Coll.)

4.3   Great Britain. Foreign Office.
       [Confidential print, Tibet and Mongolia, 1903-1923].
       London : Public Record Office, [1978?].
       4 reels.

       MFILM N.S. 1734   MTXT

4.32   Great Britain. Foreign Office.
       Report by Mr. C. W. Campbell, His Majesty's consul at Wuchow, on a journey in Mongolia.   London : HMSO, 1904.

       DS793.M7G79   HOV (Sokolsky Coll.)

4.34   Great Britain. Public Record Office.
          General correspondence. Political: China, 1906-   .
        [London, 1970-   ].
           627 reels.

                LIBRARY HAS: Reels 18-41 (1906), 207-233 (1907), 408-435
                  (1908), 612-643 (1909), 842-875 (1910), 1062-1099
                  (1911), 1310-1349 (1912), 1590-1629 (1913), 1924-1950
                  (1914), 2298-2342 (1915), 2644-2659 (1916), 2904-2921
                  (1917), 3173-3191 (1918), 3680-3703 (1919), 5295-5349
                  (1920), 6582-6670 (1921), 7970-8040 (1922)
               MFILM N.S. 730   MTXT

4.35   Great Britain. Foreign Office.
          [Private collections, Jordan papers, 1910-19]
        London : Public Record Office, [1976?].
           4 reels.

               MFILM N.S. 1737   MTXT

4.36   The Opium trade, 1910-1941.   Wilmington, Del. : Scholarly
          Resources, [1974].
           6 v.

           "A facsimile reproduction of the Foreign Office Collection
        (F.O. 415) in the Public Record Office, London."
           Contents: v.1, 1910-1911.--v.2, 1912.--v.3, 1913-1916.--
        v.4, 1917-1921.--v.5, 1922-1926.--v.6, 1927-1941.

               HV5816.O6   GOV

4.38   Great Britain. Foreign Office.
          Correspondence respecting the cultivation of opium in China.
        London : HMSO, 1921.

               Brit.Doc. C1921 v.42   GOV

4.4   Great Britain. Foreign Office.
          [Embassy and consular archives, China, Shanghai supreme
        court, Yunnan opium case, 1916].   [London] : Public Record
        Office, 1972.
           1 reel.

               MFILM N.S. 1739   MTXT

4.42   Great Britain. Foreign Office.
            Correspondence respecting the affairs of China.   London :
         HMSO, [1912].
            2 v.

                Brit.Doc. C1912 v.121   GOV

4.422   Great Britain. Foreign Office.
            Further correspondence respecting the affairs of China.
         London : HMSO, 1913-14.

                Brit.Doc. C1914 v.101   GOV

4.44   Great Britain. Foreign Office. Historical Section.
            Kiaochow and Weihaiwei.   London : HMSO, 1920.

                940.008.G786 v.12   STK

4.46   Great Britain. Foreign Office. Historical Section.
            Macao.   London : HMSO, 1920.

                940.008.G786 v.13   STK

4.48   Great Britain. Foreign Office. Historical Section.
            Mongolia.   London : HMSO, 1920.

                940.008.G786 v.12   STK

4.5   Great Britain. Foreign Office. Historical Section.
            Tibet.   London : HMSO, 1920.

                940.008.G786 v.12   STK

4.52   Great Britain. Foreign Office.
            [Embassy and consular archives, China, Shanghai, Boxer
         indemnity: re-allocation to Chinese education development,
         1923-38].   London : Public Record Office, 1972.
            3 reels.

                MFILM N.S. 1738   MTXT

4.54   Great Britain. Foreign Office.
            Papers respecting labour conditions in China.
         London : HMSO, 1925.

                Brit.Doc. 1924-25 v.30   GOV

4.56   Great Britain. Foreign Office. Chinese Indemnity Advisory
       Committee.
       Report of the advisory committee together with other
documents respecting the China indemnity.   London : HMSO,
1926.

       Brit.Doc. C1926 v.8   GOV

MISCELLANEOUS BRITISH GOVERNMENT SOURCES

5.1   Great Britain. War Office. General Staff.
       Military report on the province of Chiang-su (north of the
Yang-tzu)...corrected to August, 1910.   London : HMSO, 1911.

       DS793.K5G78   HOV

5.12   Great Britain. Dept. of Overseas Trade.
       Report on the industrial and economic situation of China.
London, 1920-   .

       Title varies: 1919, Report on the conditions and prospects of
British trade with China; 1921, General report on the
commercial, industrial and economic situation of China; 1922,
Report on the commercial, industrial and economic situation of
China; 1929, Economic conditions in China; 1931/32, Trade and
economic conditions in China; 1935/37, Report on economic and
commercial conditions in China.

       LIBRARY HAS: 1920; 1922-28; 1930; 1933; 1935
       380.005.G786   STK

5.14   Great Britain. Parliament. House of Commons.
       Sessional papers.   [London : HMSO].

       The parliamentary sessional papers include, among vast
amounts of other material, authoritative information on
political, economic, diplomatic and other relations between
China and Great Britain.
       Includes cumulative indexes.

       LIBRARY HAS: 1805-
       J301.K63   GOV

       LIBRARY HAS: 1801-1900//
       MFICHE 446   GOV

       LIBRARY HAS: 1980-
       MFICHE 353   GOV

5.16   Great Britain. Parliament. House of Lords.
            Sessional papers. [London : HMSO].

        The parliamentary sessional papers include, among vast
        amounts of other material, authoritative information on
        political, economic, diplomatic and other relations between
        China and Great Britain.
            Includes cumulative indexes.

            LIBRARY HAS: [1803-   ]
            J301.J6 GOV

U.S. DIPLOMATIC RECORDS

6.1   U.S. Consulate, Canton, China.
            Despatches from United States consuls in Canton, 1790-1906.
        Washington : National Archives, 1947.
            20 reels.

            MFILM N.S. 715 MTXT

6.12   U.S. Dept. of State.
            Diplomatic instructions of the Department of State,
        1801-1906. Washington : National Archives, 1945-46.

            Partial contents: Reels 38-43, China.

            MFILM N.S. 908 MTXT

6.14   U.S. Legation (China)
            Records of the United States Legation in China, 1843-1945.
        Washington : National Archives, 1963.
            20 reels.

            MFILM N.S. 714 MTXT

6.16   U.S. Dept. of State.
            Despatches from United States ministers to China, 1843-1906.
        Washington : National Archives, 1958.
            131 reels.

            MFILM N.S. 707 MTXT

6.18   U.S. Consulate, Amoy, China.
            Despatches from United States consuls in Amoy, 1844-1906.
        Washington : National Archives, 1947.
            15 reels.

            MFILM N.S. 726 MTXT

6.2   U.S. Consulate, Hong Kong.
          Despatches from United States consuls in Hong Kong,
        1844-1906. Washington : National Archives, 1947.
          21 reels.

             MFILM N.S. 712 MTXT

6.22   U.S. Consulate, Shanghai, China.
          Despatches from United States consuls in Shanghai, 1847-1906.
        Washington : National Archives, 1947.
          53 reels.

             MFILM N.S. 723 MTXT

6.24   U.S. Consulate, Foochow, China.
          Despatches from United States consuls in Foochow, 1849-1906.
        Washington : National Archives, 1947.
          10 reels.

             MFILM N.S. 701 MTXT

6.26   U.S. Consulate, Macao.
          Despatches from United States consuls in Macao, 1849-1896.
        Washington : National Archives, 1947.
          2 reels.

             MFILM N.S. 710 MTXT

6.28   U.S. Consulate, Ningpo, China.
          Despatches from United States consuls in Ningpo, 1853-1896.
        Washington : National Archives, 1947.
          7 reels.

             MFILM N.S. 724 MTXT

6.3   U.S. Consulate, Swatow, China.
          Despatches from United States consuls in Swatow, 1860-1881.
        Washington : National Archives, 1947.
          4 reels.

             MFILM N.S. 713 MTXT

6.32   U.S. Consulate, Hankow, China.
          Despatches from United States consuls in Hankow, 1861-1906.
        Washington : National Archives, 1947.
          8 reels.

             MFILM N.S. 719 MTXT

6.34 U.S. Consulate, Chefoo, China.
      Despatches from United States consuls in Chefoo, 1863-1906.
   Washington : National Archives, 1947.
      9 reels.

         MFILM N.S. 716 MTXT

6.36 U.S. Consulate, Chinkiang, China.
      Despatches from United States consuls in Chinkiang,
   1865-1902. Washington : National Archives, 1947.
      7 reels.

         MFILM N.S. 717 MTXT

6.38 U.S. Consulate, Tientsin, China.
      Despatches from United States consuls in Tientsin, 1868-1906.
   Washington : National Archives, 1947.
      8 reels.

         MFILM N.S. 721 MTXT

6.4   U.S. Consulate, Chungking, China.
      Despatches from United States consuls in Chungking,
   1896-1906. Washington : National Archives, 1947.
      1 reel.

         MFILM N.S. 702 MTXT

6.42 U.S. Consulate, Tan-Shui, Formosa.
      Despatches from United States consuls in Tamsui, 1898-1906:
   register, 1898-1906, and volume 1, July 22, 1898-August 7,
   1906. Washington : National Archives, 1947.
      1 reel.

         MFILM N.S. 4016 MTXT

6.44 U.S. Consulate, Nanking, China.
      Despatches from United States consuls in Nanking, 1902-1906.
   Washington : National Archives, 1947.
      1 reel.

         MFILM N.S. 722 MTXT

6.46   U.S. Consulate, Antung, China.
        Despatches from United States consuls in Antung, 1904-1906.
    Washington : National Archives, 1957.
        1 reel.

        MFILM N.S. 708   MTXT

6.48   U.S. Consulate, Hangchow, China.
        Despatches from United States consuls in Hangchow, 1904-1906.
    Washington : National Archives, 1947.
        1 reel.

        MFILM N.S. 718   MTXT

6.5   U.S. Consulate, Kunming, China.
        Records of the United States Consulate in Kunming, 1922-28.
    Washington : National Archives, 1959.
        19 reels.

        MFILM N.S. 720   MTXT

U.S. CENTRAL INTELLIGENCE AGENCY MATERIAL

7.1   CIA research reports: China, 1946-1976.   Frederick, Md. :
        University Publications of America, 1982.
        6 reels.

        MFILM N.S. 3829   MTXT

7.102   Lester, Robert.
        China, 1946-1976: [Guide].   Frederick, Md. : University
    Publications of America, c1982.

        DS777.55.L4 1982   GOV

7.12   U.S. Central Intelligence Agency.
        Research aids on the People's Republic of China.
    Washington, 1973-   .

        Consists of CIA research aids dealing with economics,
    resources and trade in the PRC.
        Table of contents of each reel at head of reel.

            LIBRARY HAS: 1973-77 (28 v. on 3 reels)
        MFILM HC427.1.U52   HOV

U.S. STATE DEPT. MATERIAL

8.1 U.S. Dept. of State.
Notes to foreign legations in the United States from the Department of State, 1834-1906. Washington : National Archives, 1947.

Partial contents: Reels 13-14, China.

MFILM N.S. 725 MTXT

8.12 U.S. Dept. of State.
Records of the Department of State relating to internal affairs of China, 1910-29. Washington : National Archives, 1960.
227 reels.

MFILM N.S. 896 MTXT

8.122 U.S. National Archives and Records Service.
Pamphlet accompanying Microcopy no. 329: Records of the Department of State relating to internal affairs of China, 1910-29. Washington, 1967.

CD3031.A35 M-329 Index HOV

8.124 Rozanski, Mordechai.
Records of the Department of State relating to the internal affairs of China, 1910-1929: A descriptive guide and subject index to Microcopy no. 329. Wilmington, Del. : Scholarly Resources, c1979.

DS774.R62 MTXT & GOV

8.14 U.S. Dept. of State.
Records of the Department of State relating to political relations between China and other states, 1910-29. Washington : National Archives, 1960.
34 reels.

MFILM N.S. 897 MTXT

8.16 U.S. Dept. of State.
Records of the Department of State relating to political relations of the United States with China, 1910-29. Washington : National Archives, 1960.
2 reels.

MFILM N.S. 895 MTXT

8.18   U.S. Dept. of State.
        Extraterritoriality in China.   Washington : GPO, 1922.

           JX1570.U58 HOV

8.2   Confidential U.S. State Department Central Files: China,
        internal affairs, 1930-1939. Frederick, Md. : University
        Publications of America, c1984.
        105 reels.

           MFILM N.S. 3849 MTXT

8.202   Lester, Robert.
       Confidential U.S. State Department Central Files: China,
      internal affairs, 1930-1939: Guide.   Frederick, Md. :
      University Publications of America, c1984.

           DS775.7.L37 1984   GOV

8.21   Confidential U.S. State Department Central Files: China,
        internal affairs, 1940-1944. Frederick, Md. :
        University Publications of America, c1984.
        51 reels.

           MFILM N.S. 3991 MTXT

8.212   Lester, Robert.
       Confidential U.S. State Department Central files: China,
      internal affairs, 1940-1944: Guide.   Frederick, Md. :
      University Publications of America, c1985.

           DS775.7.L371 1985 MTXT & GOV

8.215   Confidential U.S. State Department Central Files: United
        States-China relations, 1940-1949. Frederick, Md. :
        University Publications of America, c1984.
        7 reels.

           MFILM N.S. 3993 MTXT

8.2152 Lester, Robert.
       Confidential U.S. State Department Central Files: United
      States-China relations, 1940-1949: Guide. Frederick, Md. :
      University Publications of America, c1985.

           E183.8.C5L42 1985 MTXT & GOV

8.22   U.S. Dept. of State.
        American diplomacy in the Far East; official press releases
        of the U.S. Department of State on the Sino-Japanese situation
        during 1938- .   New York City, 1939- .

            LIBRARY HAS: 1941
            327.735.U58   STK

8.24   U.S. Dept. of State.
        Foreign relations of the United States; diplomatic papers,
        1942-[1949] China.   Washington : GPO, 1956- .

            LIBRARY HAS: 1942-43
            JX233.A54   HOV

8.26   U.S. Dept. of State.
        United States relations with China, with special reference to
        the period 1944-1949, based on the files of the Department of
        State.   [Washington : GPO, 1949].

            327.7351.U58   STK

8.28   Confidential U.S. State Departement Central Files: China,
           internal affairs, 1945-1949.   Frederick, Md. : University
           Publications of America, c1984.
        75 reels.

            MFILM N.S. 3989   MTXT

8.282   Lester, Robert.
        Confidential U.S. State Department Central Files: China,
        internal affairs, 1945-1949: Guide.   Frederick, Md. :
        University Publications of America, c1985.

            DS775.7.L372 1985   MTXT & GOV

8.3   Confidential U.S. State Department central files: Formosa,
           internal affairs, 1945-1949.   Frederick, Md. : University
           Publications of America, 1985.
        3 reels.

            Awaiting cataloging for MTXT (ID CSUG86-B24795)

8.302   Schipper, Martin.
    A guide to Confidential U.S. State Department central files: Formosa, internal affairs, 1945-1945.   Frederick, Md. : University Publications of America, 1985.

    Awaiting cataloging for MTXT and GOV (ID CSUG86-09792)

MISCELLANEOUS U.S. GOVERNMENT SOURCES

9.1   Commission on Extraterritorial Jurisdiction in China.
    Report of the Commission on Extraterritoriality in China, Peking, September 16, 1926...   Washington : GPO, 1926.

    Brit.Doc. C1926 v.8   GOV

9.11   U.S. military intelligence reports: China, 1911-1941.
    Frederick, Md. : University Publications of America, [1983?].
    15 reels and guide.

    Awaiting cataloging for MTXT (ID CSUG83-B20580)

9.115 Marshall's mission to China, December 1945-January 1947; the report and appended documents.   Arlington, Va. : University Publications of America, 1976.
    2 v.

    Includes an introduction by Lyman P. van Slyke.

    E183.8.C5M35   STK

9.12   China's economy and foreign trade / U.S. Dept. of Commerce, Industry and Trade Administration, Office of East-West Country Affairs. 1977/78- . Washington : The Office, [1978-].

    Vols. for 1979/81- issued by the International Trade Administration.
    Continues: Chinese economy and foreign trade perspective.

    LIBRARY HAS: 1977/78-1979/81
    HF3836.5.U53a   GSB

9.14   U.S. Office of Strategic Services.
       China and India. Washington : University Publications of America, 1977.
       11 reels.

           MFILM N.S. 2693 MTXT
           D753.C45 GOV & MTXT (Guide)

9.145 China and India: 1950-1969 supplement / edited by Paul Kesaris. Washington : University Publications of America, c1979.
       5 reels and guide.

           Awaiting cataloging for MTXT

MISCELLANEOUS SOURCES

10.1   Davids, Jules, comp.
       American diplomatic and public papers: The United States and China. Series I: The treaty system and the Taiping Rebellion, 1842-1860. Wilmington, Del. : Scholarly Resources, [c1973].
       21 v.

           Contents: v. 1. The Kearny and Cushing missions.--v. 2. Treaty of Wanghia.--v. 3. The Canton City question and U.S. relations with the European powers.--v. 4. The Marshall mission.-- v. 5. The McLane mission.--v. 6. The Parker Mission.--v. 7. The Taiping Rebellion.--v. 8-11. Extraterritoriality.--v. 12. Formosa.--v. 13. The Arrow War.--v. 14. The Reed mission.--v. 15. The treaties of Tientsin.--v. 16. The Ward mission.--v. 17. The coolie trade and Chinese emigration.--v. 18. Trade, currency, and the opium traffic.--v. 19. Consular affairs and trade reports: Canton and Shanghai.--v. 20. Consular affairs and trade reports: Amoy, Foochow, Hong Kong, Macao, and Ningpo.--v. 21. Calendar and guide.

           E183.8.C5D29 STK

10.11 Presbyterian Church in the USA. Board of Foreign Missions.
       Correspondence and reports [on China], 1837-1911.
       Philadelphia, Pa. : Presbyterian Historical Society.
       52 reels.

           Awaiting cataloging for MTXT

10.12　Clyde, Paul Hibbert.
　　　United States policy toward China: Diplomatic and public documents, 1839-1939.

　　　　JX1428.C6C5　STK

10.14　Williams, Samuel Wells.
　　　Williams (Samuel Wells), Family papers. [New Haven, Conn. : Yale University Library, 1970].
　　　1 reel.

　　　Subtitle: Correspondence and related papers 1853-1854, in English and Chinese, of Samuel Wells Williams, missionary, diplomat, and sinologue, concerning his service as interpreter on Commodore Matthew C. Perry's expedition to Japan.

　　　　MFILM N.S. 3746　MTXT

10.16　American diplomatic and public papers: The United States and China. Series II, the United States, China, and imperial rivalries, 1861-1893.
　　　18 v.

　　　　E183.8.C5A72　STK

10.18　France. Ministere des Affaires Etrangeres.
　　　Documents diplomatiques. Chine. Paris : Imprimerie nationale.

　　　　LIBRARY HAS: 1894-1901
　　　　327.44.F822　STK

10.2　American diplomatic and public papers: The United States and China. Series III, the Sino-Japanese War to the Russo-Japanese War, 1894-1905. Wilmington, Del. : Scholarly Resources, 1981.
　　　14 v.

　　　　E183.8.C5A723　STK

10.22　France. Ministere des Affaires Etrangeres.
　　　Documents diplomatiques. Evacuation de Shanghai. 1900-1903. Paris : Imprimerie nationale, 1903.

　　　With its Documents diplomatiques. Chine, 1898-1899.

　　　　327.44.F822　STK

10.24   Wilbur, Clarence Martin, ed.
        Documents on communism, nationalism, and Soviet advisers in
        China, 1918-1927; papers seized in the 1927 Peking raid.
        New York : Columbia University Press, 1956.

            DS777.47.W56   STK

10.26   The China year book. 1912- .   Shanghai [etc.] : North China
        Daily News & Herald [etc.].

            No vols. published for 1915, 1917-18, 1920, 1933, 1937.

                LIBRARY HAS: 1912-19; 1921/22-1926; 1928-39
            JQ1501.A16   HOV (EAC)

10.28   Crothers, George Edward.
        Papers, 1885-1957.

            Partial contents: U.S. relations with the Republic of China
        (ca. 1920-40).
            Unpublished register in the library.

            St36   Mss Dept.

10.3   Finance and commerce. v. 1-38, no. 23; 1920-Dec. 1941?.
        Shanghai.

            Title varies: v.1-12, China and Far East finance and
        commerce.

            MFILM N.S. 2318   MTXT

10.32   The China weekly chronicle. v. 1-10, no. 20 (no. 1-263);
        Nov. 6, 1932-Nov. 17, 1937.   Peking.

            "Weekly edition of the Peking Chronicle."

                LIBRARY HAS: v.1-20, 1932-37//
                    WANTING: v.7:13,19,23 (1936); v.8:19,25 (1936);
                        v.9:12-14 (1937); v.10:8-10,15-16 (1937)
                079.51.C54   STK

10.34 Yang, Kuang-sheng, ed.
    The Sino-Japanese conflict and the League of Nations, 1937; speeches, documents, press comments / edited by C. Kuangson Young... Geneva : Press Bureau of the Chinese Delegation, [1937].
    Cover title: The Conflict in the Far East.

    951.324.Y22 STK

10.36 China yearbook. 1937/43-1980. Taipeh, Taiwan [etc.] : China Pub. Co. [etc.]

    Publication suspended 1947-49.
    Title varies: 1937/43-1956/57, China handbook.
    Issues for 1937/43-1937/45 compiled by the Chinese Ministry of Information.

    LIBRARY HAS: 1937/44-1980//
    DS777.53.C552 HOV

10.38 The People's Republic of China, 1949-1979: A documentary survey / edited by Harold C. Hinton. Wilmington, Del. : Scholarly Resources, 1980.
    5 v.

    Contents: v. 1. 1949-1957, From liberation to crisis.--v. 2. 1957-1965, The Great Leap Forward and its aftermath.--v. 3. 1965-1967, The Cultural Revolution.--v. 4. 1967-1968, The Cultural Revolution, part II.--v. 5. 1968-1979, After the Cultural Revolution.

    DS777.55.P4243 STK

10.4 India (Republic) Ministry of External Affairs.
    Notes, memoranda and letters exchanged and agreements signed between the Governments of India and China. White paper.
    no. [1]- ; 1954- . [New Delhi, 1954-].

    LIBRARY HAS: no.1-7, 9-10, 14 (1954-Apr. 1968)
    327.5451.I39n STK

10.42 Communist China. 1955-1971.
    Kowloon, Hong Kong : Union Research Institute.

    Vol. for 1959 is a special report for the years 1949-1959.

    LIBRARY HAS: 1958-71//
    DS777.55.C64 STK

10.44 China: Special studies, 1970-1980.   Frederick, Md. :
      University Publications of America, 1981.
      8 reels.

           MFILM N.S. 2698 MTXT
           DS777.55.K47 GOV & MTXT (Guide)

Source Materials on Japan and on Relocation of Japanese-Americans
During World War II

JAPANESE GOVERNMENT SOURCES ON FOREIGN RELATIONS

11.1   Japan. Taishikan (U.S.)
Notes from the Japanese Legation in the United States to the Department of State, 1858-1906. Washington : National Archives, 1949.
9 reels.

    MFILM N.S. 1261 MTXT

11.12   Japan. Foreign Office.
Correspondence regarding the negotiations between Japan and Russia. (1903-1904). [Washington, D.C. : Gibson Bros., 1904].

    327.52.J35 STK

11.14   Japan. Treaties, etc.
Traites et conventions entre l'Empire du Japon et les puissances etrangeres. Tokyo : Z. P. Maruya et Cie., 1908.

    341.252.J35 STK

11.16   Japan. Board of Information.
Official announcements concerning foreign relations. [Tokyo].

    LIBRARY HAS: 1941
    DS845.J34 HOV

11.18   Japan. Imperial General Headquarters.
Communiques issued by the Imperial general headquarters from December 8, 1941 to June 30, 1943. [Osaka : Mainichi Publ. Co., 1943].

    D767.J35 HOV

11.2   Japan. Gaimusho. Division of Special Records.
Documents concerning the Allied occupation and control of Japan. [Tokyo], 1949- .

    English and Japanese.
    Partial contents: v.1. Basic documents.--v.2. Political, military and cultural.--v.3. Financial, economic and reparations.

    LIBRARY HAS: v.1-6, 1949-51
    DS889.J342 HOV

11.22   Japan. Gaimusho. Johobu.
   Collection of official foreign statements on Japanese peace treaty.   [Tokyo, 195 -].

   Partial contents: v.2. From Sept.14, 1950-May 25, 1951.--v.3. From May 28, 1951-Aug.22, 1951.

   LIBRARY HAS: v.2-3
   D814.8.J356

11.24   Japan. Gaimusho. Joho Bunkakyoku.
   Diplomatic bluebook.   [Tokyo].

   LIBRARY HAS: 1970/71; 1972-77; 1980-
   DS845.J16b   STK

JAPANESE GOVERNMENT SOURCES ON ECONOMIC CONDITIONS

12.1   Japan. Dept. of Finance.
   Financial and economic annual of Japan.   Tokyo.

   Title varies: 1901, Financial annual of Japan; 1902-05, Financial and economical annual.

   LIBRARY HAS: no.2-40, 1902-40
   336.52.J35   STK

12.12   Japan. Okurasho.
   Nihon gaikoku boeki geppyo. Monthly return of the foreign trade of Japan.   1940-1961.   [Tokyo].

   Continues its Gaikoku boeki geppyo. Monthly return of the foreign trade.
   English and Japanese. Issues for 1940- lack English title. Publication suspended 1944-49?
   Continued by its Nihon boeki geppyo: himbetsu kokubetsu. Japan exports & imports: Commodity by country.

   LIBRARY HAS: Feb-Dec. 1950; Jan-Sept. 1951; 1952-61
     LIBRARY LACKS: Oct. 1956; Oct-Nov. 1957
   382.52.J35   STK

12.14   Japan. Keizai Kikakucho.
        Japanese economic statistics. Bulletin.   Sept. 1946-Sept.?
        1958.   [Tokyo].

        Issued through Oct. 1951 by the Supreme Commander for the
        Allied Powers, Economic and Scientific Section; Nov. 1951-Apr.
        1952 by the Economic Stabilization Board of Japan; May 1952-May
        1955 by the agency under its earlier name, Economic Counsel
        Board.
        Superseded by Japanese economic statistics. Bulletin. Rev.
        ed.

            LIBRARY HAS: [no.1-101, 1958-67//]
            330.952.S958   STK

12.16   Foreign trade of Japan.   Tokyo.

        Issued 19 -   by the Ministry of International Trade and
        Industry of Japan.
        Published 19 -   by the Japan Export Trade Promotion Agency
        (called 19 -   Japan Export Trade Research Organization).
        Title varies: 19 -   Japanese foreign trade.

            LIBRARY HAS: 1950; 1954; 1966/68; 1968; 1970-
            HF251.A36   STK

12.18   Economic survey of Japan.   Tokyo.

        Vols. for   -1951/52 issued by Japan Economic Stabilization
        Board; 1952/53-   by the Economic Counsel Board.
        Title varies: -1949/50, Report on current economy; Japan's
        economy under stabilization program.

            LIBRARY HAS: 1950/51-1954/55; 1956/57-1969/70; 1971/72;
              1976/77-
            HC461.E3   STK

12.2   Japan. Okurasho. Daijin Kambo. Chosabu.
        Bulletin of financial statistics.   June 1952-2d qtr., 1982.
        Tokyo.

        Supersedes its Statistical abstract of Japanese finance.

            LIBRARY HAS: 1952-71; [1972]; 1973-82//
            336.52.J39   STK

12.22　Japan. Keizai Kikakucho.
　　　　Monthly economic report.　Tokyo.

　　　　　　LIBRARY HAS: July 1952-Sept. 1965
　　　　　　　LIBRARY LACKS: Aug. 1961; May 1964
　　　　　330.952.J26　STK

12.24　Japan. Keizai Kikakucho.
　　　　Japanese economic statistics. Bulletin. Rev. ed.
　　　Oct. 1958-　.　[Tokyo].

　　　　Supersedes its Japanese economic statistics. Bulletin.

　　　　　　LIBRARY HAS: 1-101, 1958-67//
　　　　　330.952.S958a　STK

12.26　Japan. Okurasho.
　　　　General survey of the Japanese economy.　[Tokyo].

　　　　　　LIBRARY HAS: 1953/54-1956/57
　　　　　336.52.J35g　STK

12.28　Japan. Gaimusho.
　　　　Statistical survey of economy of Japan.　[Tokyo?] : Ministry
　　　of Foreign Affairs.

　　　　　　GREEN HAS: 1967-71; 1974-
　　　　　HC461.A345　STK

　　　　　　HOOVER HAS: 1954; 1962; 1968-70; 1973
　　　　　HC462.A434　HOV

　　　　　　GSB HAS: 1953; 1957; 1962; 1966-71; 1973-
　　　　　HC461.S78　GSB

12.3　Japan. Okurasho.
　　　　Nihon boeki geppyo: himbetsu kokubetsu. Japan exports &
　　　imports: Commodity by country. no. 144-　; 1962-nen
　　　1-gatsu -　.　[Tokyo] : Nihon Kanzei Kyokai.

　　　　Continues its Nihon gaikoku boeki geppyo.

　　　　　　LIBRARY HAS: 1962-64; 1967-69; 1974-
　　　　　HF251.A15　STK

12.32   Statistics on Japanese industries. 1965- .
        Tokyo : Ministry of International Trade and Industry.

    Vols. for   prepared by the Research and Statistics Dept.
(called 19 -69, Research and Statistics Division), Minister's
Secretariat, Ministry of International Trade and Industry.
    Title varies: 1965, Industries of Japan.

        LIBRARY HAS: 1966-70; 1974-
        HC462.5.S8 STK

12.34   Nihon boeki geppyo: kokubetsu himbetsu. Japan exports &
        imports: Country by commodity. 1965- .
        Tokyo : Nihon Kanzei Kyokai; Japan Tariff Association.

    Edited by Okurasho.
    Continues: Nihon boeki nempyo: kokubetsu himbetsu. Annual
return of the foreign trade of Japan: Country by commodity.

        LIBRARY HAS: 1969; 1974; 1982-
        HF251.J33 STK

12.36   White papers of Japan. [Tokyo] : Japan Institute of
        International Affairs.

    "Abstract of official reports and statistics of the Japanese
Government."

        LIBRARY HAS: 1969/70-
        HC461.W55 STK/REF

MISCELLANEOUS JAPANESE GOVERNMENT SOURCES

13.1   Japan. Laws, statutes, etc.
        Japanese government documents, 1867-1889 / edited by W. W.
        McLaren... Tokyo : [Asiatic Society of Japan], 1914.

        065.A832 v.42, pt.1 STK

13.12   Japan. Sorifu. Tokeikyoku.
        Resume statistique de l'empire du Japon. Tokio, 188 -19 .

        LIBRARY HAS: no.3-8; 10-29; 31; 33-36; 38-49; 53-54
        315.2.J351 STK

13.14   Japan. Dept. of Agriculture and Commerce.
          Statistical report.   [Tokyo?].

    Japanese and English.

        LIBRARY HAS: no.21, 1905/06; no.32, 1915; no.34, 1917
        315.2.J353   STK

13.16   Japan. Dept. of Agriculture and Commerce.
          The statistics of agriculture, industries and commerce.
        [1919]-1923.   [Tokyo] : Section of Statistics, Department of
        Agriculture and Commerce, 1921-25.

        Continued by: Statistics of the Department of commerce and
        industry; and Statistical abstract of the Department of
        agriculture and forestry (630.652.J34s   STK).
          Title varies: 1919-21, Agricultural and commercial
        statistics.

        LIBRARY HAS: 1919-21
        315.2.J36   STK

13.18   Iwado, Zenchi Tamotsu, trans.
          Japan's wartime legislation, 1939 / translated by Z. Tamotsu
        Iwado.   Tokyo : The Japan Times & Mail, [1939?].

        "The present selection of Japanese wartime legislation
        includes practically all laws enacted at the 1938-39 session of
        the Imperial diet and ordinances issued later on their bases.
        However, laws of only transient character and those of purely
        native interest have been omitted."--Preface.

        JQ1630.1939 I96   HOV

13.2   Japan.
          Official gazette. English ed.   no. [1]-1828, Apr. 4, 1946-
        Apr. 28, 1952; Sept. 1953-   .   [Tokyo] : Government Printing
        Bureau.

        Some numbers accompanied by "extra" numbers (354.52.J35a
        STK)

        LIBRARY HAS: v.1:1-20, 24-59; v.2:1-39; no.623-1828;
          May 1948-Apr. 28, 1952; Sept. 1953-
          LIBRARY LACKS: no.630, 677, 792, 946, 1041, 1178
        354.52.J35   STK

13.22   Japan. Sorifu. Tokeikyoku.
        Statistical abstract of Japan. 1950- . [Tokyo].

        Abstract edition of the Japan statistical yearbook issued by
        the Statistics Bureau of the Prime Minister's Office.

            LIBRARY HAS: 1950; 1975
            315.2.J352 STK

13.24   Japan. Sorifu. Tokeikyoku.
        Statistical handbook of Japan. [Tokyo].

            LIBRARY HAS: 1958; 1964-65; 1967; 1969-
            HA1831.A4 STK

13.26   Japan. Sorifu. Tokeikyoku.
        Monthly statistics of Japan. July 1961- . [Tokyo].

        Continues its Monthly bulletin of statistics.

            LIBRARY HAS: 1, 1961-
            315.2.J352ms STK

BRITISH FOREIGN OFFICE MATERIAL

14.1   Great Britain. Public Record Office.
            General correspondence: Japan, 1856-1905. Wilmington,
        Del. : Scholarly Resources, 1975.
            375 reels in 374.

        "Reel 53 is a duplicate of Reel 2."

            MFILM N.S. 1316 MTXT

14.102 British Foreign Office Japan correspondence, 1856-1905.
            Indexes and guides to the Scholarly Resources microfilm
            edition of the Public Record Office collection...
            Wilmington, Del. : Scholarly Resources, [1975].

            DA47.9.J3B75 GOV

14.12   Great Britain. Public Record Office.
            Confidential print: Japan, 1859-1937. [London, 1972].
            13 reels.

            MFILM N.S. 974 MTXT

14.14　Gubbins, John Harington.
　　　Japan.　London : HMSO, 1920.

　　　　940.008.G786 v.12　STK

14.16　Great Britain. Foreign Office.
　　　British Foreign Office Japan correspondence, 1856-1940.
　　London : Microfilmed for Scholarly Resources by the Public
　　Record Office, 1976.
　　　66 reels.

　　　Title on container: British Foreign Office Japan
　　correspondence, 1930-1940.

　　　　MFILM N.S. 3384　MTXT

14.162　British Foreign Office Japan correspondence, 1930-1940:
　　　Guide to the Scholarly Resources microfilm edition of the
　　　Public Record Office Collection (Text F.O. 371).

　　　　DA47.9.J3B752 1978　MTXT & GOV

14.18　Great Britain. Foreign Office.
　　　General correspondence. Political: Japan, 1906-　.
　　Wilmington, Del. : Scholarly Resources, 1976-　.

　　　For contents consult users' guides: British Foreign Office
　　Japan correspondence, 1930-1940; and British Foreign Office
　　Japan correspondence, 1941-1945.

　　　　LIBRARY HAS: 1930-45 (114 reels)
　　　　MFILM N.S. 3384　MTXT

14.2　Great Britain. Foreign Office.
　　　British Foreign Office Japan correspondence, 1856-1940.
　　London : Microfilmed for Scholarly Resources by the Public
　　Record Office, 1978.
　　　48 reels.

　　　Title on container: British Foreign Office Japan
　　correspondence, 1941-1945.

　　　　MFILM N.S. 3385　MTXT

14.202 British Foreign Office Japan correspondence, 1941-1945.
Guide to the Scholarly Resources microfilm edition of the Public Record Office collection (Text F.O. 371).
Wilmington, Del. : Scholarly Resources, 1980 (1983 printing).

    DA47.9.J3B753 1983 GOV

MISCELLANEOUS BRITISH GOVERNMENT SOURCES

15.1 Great Britain. War Office.
The Russo-Japanese war. Reports from British officers attached to the Japanese and Russian forces in the field.
London : HMSO, 1908.
3 v.

    952.3.G786 STK

15.12 Great Britain. Dept. of Overseas Trade.
Report on the commercial, industrial and financial situation in Japan.   London, 1920-   .

Title varies slightly.

    LIBRARY HAS: 1920; 1923-24; 1926; 1928-30; 1933; 1935-36
    380.005.G786 STK

15.14 Great Britain. Board of Trade.
Japan; economic and commercial conditions in Japan.
London : HMSO.

    LIBRARY HAS: 1952
    380.005.G786aj STK

U.S. DIPLOMATIC RECORDS

16.1 U.S. Dept. of State.
Diplomatic instructions of the Department of State, 1801-1906. Washington : National Archives, 1945-1946.

Partial contents: Reels 104-108, Japan.

    MFILM N.S. 908 MTXT

16.12 U.S. Dept. of State.
    Notes to foreign legations in the United States from the Department of State, 1834-1906. Washington : National Archives, 1947.

    Partial contents: Reels 66-67, Japan.

        MFILM N.S. 725 MTXT

16.14 U.S. Dept. of State.
    Despatches from United States ministers to Japan, 1855-1906. Washington : National Archives, 1949.
        82 reels.

    Arranged chronologically; first reel contains calendar.

        MFILM N.S. 1263 MTXT

16.16 U.S. Dept. of State.
    Despatches from United States consuls in Hakodate, 1856-1878. Washington : National Archives, National Archives and Records Service, General Services Administration, 1969.
        1 reel.

    "Register 1856-1878 and despatches volumes 1 and 2, July 15, 1856-Aug. 20, 1878."

        MFILM N.S. 4001
        E183.8.J3D47 1973 MTXT (Guide)

16.18 U.S. Consulate, Nagasaki, Japan.
    Despatches from United States consuls in Nagasaki, 1860-1906. Washington : National Archives, 1948.
        7 reels.

        MFILM N.S. 4020 MTXT

16.2 U.S. Consulate, Kobe, Japan.
    Despatches from United States consuls in Osaka and Hiogo (Kobe), 1868-1906. Washington : National Archives and Records Service, General Services Administration, 1969.
        6 reels.

        MFILM N.S. 4021 MTXT

16.22   U.S. Consulate General, Yokohama, Japan.
           Despatches from United States consuls in Yokohama, 1897-1906.
        Washington : National Archives, 1948.
           5 reels.

              MFILM N.S. 4019   MTXT

16.24   Confidential U.S. diplomatic post records: Japan, 1914-   /
           edited by Paul Kesaris.   Frederick, Md. : University
           Publications of America, 1983-   .

              Contents: pt.1. 1914-18 (11 reels).--pt.2. 1919-29 (50
           reels).--pt.3, sect.A. 1930-35 (25 reels).--pt.3, sect.B.
           1936-41 (56 reels, numbered 1-22, 22A-55).

                 LIBRARY HAS: pt.1-2; pt.3, sect.A-B
              MFILM N.S. 3247   MTXT

16.242 Confidential U.S. diplomatic post records: Japan, 1914-   .
           Guide / compiled by Robert Lester.   Frederick, Md. :
           University Publications of America, 1983-   .

              Contents: pt.1. 1914-18.--pt.2. 1919-29.--pt.3. 1930-41.

                 LIBRARY HAS: pt.1-3
              E183.8.J3C66 1983   MTXT

U.S. STATE DEPT. MATERIAL

17.1   U.S. Dept. of State.
           The policy of the United States and Japan in the Far East.
        New York City : American Branch of the Association for
        International Conciliation, 1908.

              341.6.A849 no.12   STK

17.12   U.S. Dept. of State.
           Text of notes exchanged between the United States and
        Japanese governments regarding their policy in China, and
        declaration of the Chinese government on the subject...
        London : HMSO, 1918.

              Brit.Doc. C1917-18 v.38   GOV

17.14 U.S. Dept. of State.
Records of the Department of State relating to internal affairs of Japan, 1910-29. Washington, 1963.
43 reels.

Partial contents: Reels 1-3. Lists of documents.--4-12. Political affairs.--13. Public order and safety.--14-18. Military affairs and the Army.--19-20. Naval affairs, Navy, naval vessels.--21-24. Social matters.--25-32. Economic matters.--33-34. Industrial matters.--35-36. Communication and transportation.--37-40. Navigation.--41. Other internal affairs.--42. Formosa, Sakhalin Island (Japanese portion).--43. Kwantung leased territory.

LIBRARY HAS: Reels 1-43
CD3031.A35 M-422 HOV

17.142 U.S. National Archives and Records Service.
Records of the Department of State relating to internal affairs of Japan, 1910-29. Pamphlet accompanying Microcopy no. 422. Washington, 1965.

CD3031.A35 M-422 Index HOV REFERENCE ROOM

17.16 U.S. Dept. of State.
Records of the Department of State relating to political relations between Japan and other states, 1910-1929. Washington : National Archives, National Archives and Records Service, General Services Administration, 1963.
1 reel.

MFILM N.S. 2645 MTXT

17.18 Records of the Department of State relating to internal affairs of Japan. Washington : National Archives, National Archives and Records Service, General Services Administration, 1963- .

Title on pt.2- : Internal affairs of Japan: records of the U.S. Department of State relating to the internal affairs of Japan (Decimal file 894).

LIBRARY HAS: pt.1 (Reels 1-43); pt.2 (Reels 1-33);
   pt.3 (Reels 1-20)
MFILM N.S. 3890

17.182 Guide to records of the U.S. Department of State relating to
       the internal affairs of Japan, 1930-1939 and 1940-1944
       (Decimal file 894). Wilmington, Del. : Scholarly Resources,
       1984.

       DS885.G85 1984   MTXT & GOV

17.2   U.S. Dept. of State.
       Papers relating to the foreign relations of the United
       States. Japan: 1931-1941. Washington : GPO, 1943.
       2 v.

       JX233.A55   HOV

17.23 Confidential U.S. State Department Central Files: Japan,
       internal affairs, 1945-1949. Frederick, Md. :
       University Publications of America, c1984.
       42 reels.

       MFILM N.S. 4069   MTXT

17.232 Confidential U.S. State Department Central Files: Japan,
       internal affairs, 1945-1949. Guide. Frederick, Md. :
       University Publications of America, c1985.

       Awaiting cataloging for MTXT & GOV

17.24 U.S. Dept. of State. Office of Northeast Asian Affairs.
       United States relations with Japan, 1945-1952.
       New York : American Institute of Pacific Relations, 1953.

       E183.8.J3U58   HOV

17.26 Confidential U.S. State Department Central Files: Japan,
       internal affairs, 1950-1954. Frederick, Md. :
       University Publications of America, c1984.
       62 reels.

       MFILM N.S. 4061   MTXT

U.S. GOVERMENT SOURCES: WORLD WAR II

18.1   The MAGIC documents: Summaries and transcripts of the top
       secret diplomatic communications of Japan, 1938-1945.
       Washington : University Publications of America, c1980.
       14 reels.

       MFILM N.S. 3761   MTXT

18.102 Quist, Norm.
    A calendar to the MAGIC documents: Summaries and transcripts of the top secret diplomatic communications of Japan, 1938-1945. Washington : University Publications of America, c1980.

        D754.J3M221 1980 GOV REF

18.104 A Subject and name index to the MAGIC documents: Summaries and transcripts of the top-secret diplomatic communications of Japan, 1938-1945 / compiled by David Wallace. Frederick, Md. : University Publications of America, c1982.

        Contents: Introductory essays.--Subject and name index.

        D754.J3M22 1982 GOV REF

18.12 U.S. Dept. of State.
    Prelude to infamy; official report on the final phase of U.S.-Japanese relations October 17 to December 7, 1941. [Washington : United States News, 1943].

        E183.8.J3A3 HOV

18.14 U.S. National Archives.
    Federal records of World War II. Washington : [GPO], 1950 [i.e., 1951].
    2 v.

        Contents: v.1. Civilian agencies.--v.2. Military agencies.

        JK464 1951 A3 HOV

18.16 U.S. Office of Strategic Services.
    Japan and its occupied territories during World War II. Washington : University Publications of America, 1977.
    16 reels.

        MFILM N.S. 2695 MTXT

18.162 Japan and its occupied territories during World War II.
    [Guide]. Washington : University Publications of America, c1977.

        D767.2.J36 MTXT & GOV

18.18 U.S. Board of Economic Warfare.
    Japanese techniques of occupation; key laws and official documents / [by the] Reoccupation Division in cooperation with the Enemy Branch. [Washington], 1943.
    3 v.

    Contents: v.1. Japan proper.--v.2. Manchoukuo.--v.3. Occupied China: Inner Mongolia, North China, Central China.

    JX5003.U574   HOV

18.19 U.S. Joint Chiefs of Staff.
    Records of the Joint Chiefs of Staff: The Pacific theater, 1942-1945. Frederick, Md. : University Publications of America, [1981?].
    14 reels and guide.

    Awaiting cataloging for MTXT

18.195 Military intelligence in the Pacific, 1942-1946: Bulletins of the Intelligence Center, Pacific Ocean Area, Joint Intelligence Center, Pacific Ocean Area, and the Commander-in-Chief, Pacific and Pacific Ocean Area. Wilmington, Del. : Scholarly Resources, 1984.
    41 reels.

    MFILM N.S. 4000   MTXT

18.197 Guide to the Scholarly Resources microfilm edition of Military intelligence in the Pacific, 1942-46: Bulletins of the Intelligence Center, Pacific Ocean Area, Joint Intelligence Center, Pacific Ocean Area, and the Commander-in-Chief, Pacific and Pacific Ocean Area. Wilmington, Del. : Scholarly Resources, [1984?].

    D767.9.G84 1984   MTXT

18.2 U.S. Strategic Bombing Survey.
Records of the U.S. Strategic Bombing Survey: Pacific survey / [by the] Intelligence Branch, Library and Target Data Section. Washington : National Archives and Records Service, 1981.
20 reels.

Contains the Joint Army-Navy intelligence studies (JANIS) no. 73, 75-81, 84-87, 102-104, 150, 154-155, 157 compiled by the Office of Chief of Naval Operations, Division of Naval Intelligence and issued by the Joint Intelligence Study Publishing Board, 1944-1945.
Contents listed at head of each reel.

   MFILM CD3031.A35M1169 HOV

18.22 U.S. National Archives.
The end of the war in the Pacific. Surrender documents in facsimile... [Washington : GPO, 1945].

   940.94.J3U59 STK

18.23 Manhattan Project: Official history and documents.
Washington : University Publications of America, c1977.
12 reels.

   MFILM N.S. 3216 MTXT

18.232 A Guide to Manhattan Project: Official history and documents / edited by Paul Kesaris. Washington : University Publications of America, c1977.

   QC773.3.U5G8 1977 MTXT

18.24 U.S. Far East Command. Military Intelligence Section. Historical Division.
Statements of Japanese officials on World War II. (English translations) / [by the] U.S. Army, General Headquarters, Far East Command, Military Intelligence Service, Historical Division. Washington : Library of Congress, Photoduplication Service, [1976].
2 reels.

   MFILM N.S. 2673 MTXT
   Another copy: MFILM D767.2.U52 HOV

U.S. GOVERNMENT SOURCES: INTERNMENT OF JAPANESE-AMERICANS DURING WORLD WAR II

19.1   U.S. National Archives.
Preliminary inventory of the records of the War Relocation Authority (Record group 210) / compiled by Estelle Rebec and Martin Rogin. Washington, 1955.

"Select list of significant documents, reports, and studies."

Z1223.W35A3   HOV

19.12   U.S. Commission on Wartime Relocation and Internment of Civilians.
U.S. Commission on Wartime Relocation and Internment of Civilians: [Papers]. Frederick, Md. : University Publications of America, c1983.

Partial contents: pt.1. Numerical file archive (35 reels).

LIBRARY HAS: pt.1 (35 reels)
MFILM N.S. 3817   MTXT

19.122 Lester, Robert.
Papers of the U.S. Commission on Wartime Relocation and Internment of Civilians. [Reel index] / compiled by Robert Lester. Frederick, Md. : University Publications of America, c1984.

Partial contents: Part 1. Numerical file archive.
Includes indexes.

LIBRARY HAS: pt.1
D769.8.A6L47 1984   MTXT & GOV REF

19.14   U.S. War Dept.
Japanese evacuation from the West Coast, 1942: Final report. New York : Arno Press, 1978.

Reprint of the 1943 ed. published by the U.S. GPO.

D769.8.A6U4 1978 STK

U.S. GOVERNMENT SOURCES: POSTWAR JAPAN

20.1   U.S. Dept. of State.
Trial of Japanese war criminals. Documents: 1. Opening statement by Joseph B. Keenan, chief of counsel; 2. Charter of the International Military Tribunal for the Far East; 3. Indictment. Washington : GPO, 1946.

    JX6731.W3U62   HOV

20.11 International Military Tribunal for the Far East.
The Tokyo war crimes trial / annotated, compiled and edited by R. John Pritchard and Sonia Magbanua Zaide; project director, Donald Cameron Watt. New York : Garland Publ., 1981.
27 v.

"The complete transcript of the proceedings of the International Military Tribunal for the Far East."

    JX5438.3.P744 1981   STK

20.112 International Military Tribunal for the Far East.
The Tokyo war crimes trial. Index and guide / annotated, compiled and edited by R. John Pritchard and Sonia Magbanua Zaide; project director, Donald Cameron Watt. New York : Garland Publ., 1981.
5 v.

    JX5438.3.P744 1981 Suppl.   STK

20.12 U.S. Dept. of State.
Occupation of Japan, policy and progress. Washington : GPO, [1946].

    DS889.U59   HOV

20.14 Supreme Commander for the Allied Powers.
Summation...non-military activities in Japan... no. [1]-35; Sept/Oct. 1945-Aug. 1948.

Title varies: Summation...non-military activities in Japan and Korea.

    LIBRARY HAS: no.1-35, 1945-48//
    952.53.S957s   STK

20.16   Supreme Commander for the Allied Powers.
          Press translations and summaries, Japan.   [Tokyo?].

            LIBRARY HAS: 1945-49//
            G.D. INTL.   HOV

20.18   U.S. Dept. of the Army. Civil Affairs Division.
          Occupied Japan; a summary.   [n.p., 1949?].

          "The information is current as of 15 August, 1948."

            952.53.U58   STK

20.2   Supreme Commander for the Allied Powers. Government Section.
          Brief progress report on the political reorientation of
          Japan.   [Tokyo], 1949.

            952.53.S957ba   STK

20.22   Supreme Commander for the Allied Powers. Government Section.
          Political reorientation of Japan, September 1945 to September
          1948; report.   [Coordination, revision and editing supervised
          by Frank Rizzo, and an Index by the Library of Congress.
          Washington : GPO, 1949].
             2 v.

            Vol.2, Appendices, contains documents, declarations and laws.

            952.53.S957   STK
            Another copy: MFILM N.S. 3885   MTXT

20.24   U.S. War Dept. Civil Affairs Division.
          Weekly report on Japan.   [Tokyo].

            LIBRARY HAS: [no.76-292, 1947-51]
            G.D. USA   HOV

20.26   U.S. Naval Technical Mission to Japan.
          Reports of the U.S. Naval Technical Mission to Japan,
          1945-1946.   Wilmington, Del. : Scholarly Resources, 1983.
             13 reels.

            Contents listed at head of reel 1.

            MFILM VA653.U56 1983   HOV

MISCELLANEOUS U.S. GOVERNMENT SOURCES

21.1 U.S. Treaties, etc.
Treaties between the United States of America and China, Japan, Lewchew and Siam, Acts of Congress, and the Attorney-General's opinion, with the decrees and regulations issued for the guidance of U.S. Consular Courts in China. Hong Kong, 1862.

    JX263.U594   HOV

21.12 U.S. Treaties, etc., 1909-1913 (Taft).
Treaty and protocol between the United States and Japan. Commerce and navigation. Signed at Washington, February 21, 1911. Washington : GPO, 1913.

    341.273.U59j   STK

21.14 U.S. Treaties, etc.
Diplomatic relations between the United States and Japan, 1908-1924. Worcester, Mass. and New York City : Carnegie Endowment for International Peace, Division of Intercourse and Education, [1925].

Contents: Arbitration.--Commerce and navigation.--Immigration.--Mandates.--Policy in the Far East.

    341.6.A849 no.211   STK

21.16 U.S. State-War-Navy Coordinating Committee. Subcommittee for the Far East.
Records of the Subcommittee for the Far East, 1945-1948. Washington : National Archives and Records Service, 1975.
14 reels.

    MFILM CD3031.A35T1205   HOV

21.18 U.S. Office of Strategic Services.
Postwar Japan, Korea, and Southeast Asia. Washington : University Publications of America, 1977.
13 reels.

1950-1961 supplement has title: Japan, Korea, Southeast Asia, and the Far East generally.

    MFILM N.S. 2694   MTXT

21.182 Postwar Japan, Korea, and Southeast Asia. [Guide] / edited
by Paul Kesaris. Washington : University Publications of
America, 1977.

   Includes index.

      DS885.P68   MTXT & GOV

21.2   Japan, Korea, and the security of Asia, 1946-1976.
          Frederick, Md. : University Publications of America, c1982.
          5 reels.

   Microfilm of typescripts from the U.S. Central Intelligence
Agency.
   Accompanied by a guide: Japan, Korea, and the security of
Asia, 1946-1976 / compiled by Robert Lester.
   Includes index.

      MFILM N.S. 2874   MTXT

21.22 Japan, Korea and the security of Asia: Special studies,
          1970-1980. Frederick, Md. : University Publications
          of America, 1981.
          4 reels.

      MFILM N.S. 2697   MTXT

21.222 Kesaris, Paul.
          Japan, Korea and the security of Asia: Special studies,
          1970-1980. [Guide]. Frederick, Md. : University Publications
          of America, c1981.

      DS889.15.K47   MTXT

MISCELLANEOUS SOURCES

22.1   Perry, Matthew Calbraith.
          Narrative of the expedition of an American squadron to the
       China seas and Japan performed in the years 1852, 1853, and
       1854, under the command of Commodore M. C. Perry by order of
       the Government of the United States / compiled from the
       original notes and journals of Commodore Perry and his
       officers, at his request, and under his supervision, by Francis
       L. Hawks. Published by order of the Congress of the United
       States. Washington : B. Tucker, 1856-   .

      LIBRARY HAS: v.1-2
      DS809.P464   HOV

22.12 Beasley, William G., ed. and trans.
    Select documents on Japanese foreign policy, 1853-1868 / translated and edited by W. G. Beasley.   London and New York : Oxford University Press, 1955.

        327.52.B368   STK

22.14 The Meiji Japan through contemporary sources / compiled by the Center for East Asian Cultural Studies.   Tokyo, [1969-   ].

    Partial contents: v.1. Basic documents, 1854-1889.--v.2. 1844-1882.--v.3. 1869-1894.

        LIBRARY HAS: v.1-3
        DS881.9.M394   STK

22.16 Ch'en, Ho-hsien.
    Les relations diplomatiques entre la Chine et le Japon de 1871 a nos jours; traite, conventions, echange de lettres, etc. Paris : Editions de "La Vie universitaire," 1921.

        327.51.H825   STK

22.18 The Japan daily mail; a review of Japanese commerce, politics, literature and art. Weekly edition.   Yokohama [etc.], 1872-   .

    Title varies: 1872-Apr. 3, 1915, Japan weekly mail.
    Publication suspended Oct. 13, 1917-Mar. 30, 1918?
    Continued by: Japan times and mail. Weekly edition.

        LIBRARY HAS: v.3-8, 1872-77; new ser.: v.2-7, 1878-83;
          [ser. 3]: v.1-65, 1884-1917
        079.J35   STK

22.185 Saionji, Kinmochi.
    The Saionji-Harada memoirs.   [Tokyo?] : General Headquarters, United States Army Forces, Pacific Military Intelligence Section, General Staff, [1947?].
    24 v. in 6.

        (V) DS884.S3A32   HOV

22.2   The Japan chronicle. Weekly edition.   -Oct.16, 1941.   Kobe.

   Began publication in 1897.
   Title varies: 1897-1901, The Kobe chronicle.
   Running title, 1902- , The Japan weekly chronicle.

      LIBRARY HAS: [1911-14]; 1915-16; [1917]; [1922-23]
   952.05.J32   STK

22.24   The Japan year book; complete cyclopaedia of general
   information and statistics on Japan and Japanese territories.
   1st-27th year; 1905-31.   Tokyo : The Japan Year Book Office,
   1905-[31].

   Superseded by Japan-Manchoukuo year book.

      LIBRARY HAS: 1, 1905; 3-27, 1907-31//
   315.2.J34   STK

22.26   Kinai, M., comp.
      The Russo-Japanese war (official reports).   (English
   translations are from "Japan Times") / compiled by M. Kinai.
   Tokyo : The Shimbashido [1905-07].
      2 v.

      952.3.K51   STK

22.28   Prussia. Armee. Grosser Generalstab. Kriegsgeschichtliche
      Abteilung.
      The Russo-Japanese war / prepared in the Historical Section
   of the German General Staff; authorized translation by Karl von
   Donat.   London : H. Rees, 1908-14.
      7 v. in 8.

      Cover title: German official account of the Russo-Japanese
   War.
      Contents: [I] The Ya-lu.--[II] Wa-Fan-Gou, and actions
   preliminary to Liao-Yan.--[III] The battle of Liao-Yan.--
   [IV] The battle on the Scha-Ho.--[V] The raid to Yin-Kou and
   the battle of San-De-Pu.--[VI] Between San-De-Pu and Mukden.--
   [VII] The battle of Mukden. pt.I From February 25 to March 3,
   1905.

      LIBRARY HAS: v.1-5
   DS516.P972   HOV

22.3   Russia. Komissia po opisaniiu russko-iaponskoi voiny 1904 i
          1905 godov.
        Russko-iaponskaia voina, 1904-1905 gg / rabota Voenno-
        istoricheskoi komissii po opisaniiu russko-iaponskoi voiny.
        S.-Peterburg : Tip. A. S. Suvorina [etc.], 1910.
          9 v. in 29.

        Contents: t.1. Sobytiia na Dal'nem Vostokie,
        predshestvovavshiia voinie, i podgotovka k etoi voinie.--
        t.2. Pervyi period (2 v.)--t.3. Liaoianskii period (2 v.)--
        t.4. Shakhz-Sandzpu (2 v.)--t.5. Mukdenskoe srazhenie (2 v.)--
        t.6. Sypingaiskii period.--t.7. Tyl dieistvuiushchei armii
        (2 v.)--t.8. Oborona Kvantuna i Port-Artura (2 v.)--t.9.
        Vtorostepennye teatry voennykh dieistvii.

            LIBRARY LACKS: Atlases
            DS516.A5   HOV

22.32   Russia. Komissia po opisaniia russko-iaponskoi voiny 1904 i
          1905 godov.
        Der russisch-japanische Krieg: Amtliche Darstellung des
        russischen Generalstabes; deutsche vom russischen
        Kriegsministerium mit Allerhöchster Genehmigung autorisierte
        Ausgabe, von Freiherr von Tettau.   Berlin : E.S. Mittler,
        1910-   . [v.1, 1911].

        Partial contents: Bd.5. Port Arthur, pt.1. Die Verteidigung
        Kwantungs bis zur engen Einschliessung der Festung.

            LIBRARY HAS: v.5, pt.1
            952.3.R968   STK

22.34   Paris Peace Conference, 1919. China.
        The Shantung question, a statement of China's claim together
        with important documents submitted to the Peace conference in
        Paris.   [San Francisco] : Chinese National Welfare Society in
        America, 1919.

            327.51.C539s   STK

22.36   Carnegie Endowment for International Peace. Division of
          International Law.
        The Sino-Japanese negotiations of 1915; Japanese and Chinese
        documents and Chinese official statement.   Washington, 1921.

            341.6.C280p no.45   STK

22.38 Mitsubishi Economic Research Institute, Tokyo.
    Monthly circular; survey of economic conditions in Japan.
    no. 1- ; 1923- . Tokyo.

    Publication suspended May 1941-May 1947.
    Issued   -Mar. 1932 by the Economic Research Dept.,
    Mitsubishi Goshi Kaisha; Apr. 1932-Apr. 1941 by the institute
    under its earlier name: Mitsubishi Economic Research Bureau.

        LIBRARY HAS: no.418, 1964; no.422, 1965-
        HC461.M5 STK/CPR

22.4 Lowe, Chuan-hua, ed.
    Official documents relating to Japan's undeclared war in
    Shanghai / compiled and edited by Lowe Chuan-hua. Shanghai :
    Chinese Chamber of Commerce, [1932].

        DS777.51.L913 HOV

22.42 League of Nations.
    Reports to the League of Nations by the Committee of
    Representatives at Shanghai of certain states members of the
    League Council appointed to report on events in Shanghai and
    neighbourhood, Shanghai, February 6 and 12, 1932. London :
    HMSO, 1932.

        Brit.Doc. C1931-32 v.27 GOV

22.44 League of Nations.
    Correspondence and resolutions respecting events in Shanghai
    and neighbourhood, February-March 1932. London : HMSO, 1932.

        Brit.Doc. C1931-32 v.27 GOV

22.46 The Japan year book. 1933- . [Tokyo] : The Foreign Affairs
    Association of Japan, [1933-].

        LIBRARY HAS: 1933; 1935-1940/41; 1943/44; 1946/48
        315.2.J342 STK

22.48   Japan trade guide, with a comprehensive mercantile directory.
          1935-   .   Tokyo : Jiji Press [etc.].

        "Compiled under the supervision of the Ministry of
        International Trade and Industry, Japanese Government,"
        1957-   .

              GREEN HAS: 1935; 1957; 1959-62
              HF3824.J35   STK

              HOOVER HAS: 1935-41; 1949; 1951; 1955-59
              HF3824.J35   HOV

22.5   Tokyo gazette; a report of current policies, official
          statements and statistics.   July 1937-   .

        Consists mainly of selections from the Weekly report, edited
        by the Bureau of Information.

              LIBRARY HAS: 1-4, 1937-41
              952.05.T646   STK

22.52   The Orient year book.   1934-   .   Tokyo : The Asia Statistics
          Co. [etc.], 1933-   .

        Title varies: 1934-41, Japan-Manchoukuo year book.
        Formed by the union of the Japan year book (1905-31) and the
        Japan times year book.

              LIBRARY HAS: 1935-43
              DS803.O69   HOV

22.54   Benda, Harry Jindrich, ed.
          Japanese military administration in Indonesia: Selected
        documents / [by] Harry J. Benda, James K. Irikura, [and] Koichi
        Kishi; translated by James K. Irikura, Margaret W. Broekhuysen,
        and Iram J. Pamoedjo.   New Haven, Ct.] : Yale University
        Southeast Studies, [1965].

              JX5003.B365   STK

22.56　Hussey, Alfred Rodman.
　　　　Hussey papers, 1945-1948.
　　　　12 reels.

　　Hussey, a lawyer, was one of the three high officials in the Government Section of SCAP (Supreme Commander for the Allied Powers) who wrote the final draft of the present constitution of Japan. He strongly advocated civil rights in advising the Japanese government and was instrumental in the establishment of the Labor Ministry. The collection contains memoranda, records, correspondence, and newspaper and journal articles dated 1945-1948.
　　A detailed checklist and an M.A. thesis by John Bowden, titled <u>SCAP files of Commander Alfrey Hussey, 1968</u>, are included at beginning of the set.

　　　　MFILM DS889.H8　HOV

22.58　International Military Tribunal for the Far East.
　　　　Special studies. no. 1-21.　[Tokyo, 1947].

　　　　MFILM JX6731.W3I61　HOV

22.6　Japan statistical yearbook. 1949- .　[Tokyo?] : Nihon Statistical Association.

　　Edited by Statistics Bureau of the Prime Minister's Office (with Executive Office of the Statistics Commission, 1949).

　　　　LIBRARY HAS: 1951-
　　　　HA1832.J36　STK/GOV

22.62　Standard trade index of Japan. 1950- .　Tokyo : Japan Chamber of Commerce and Industry.

　　Title varies: 1950-1955/56, Japan register of merchants, manufacturers & shippers.

　　　　LIBRARY HAS: 1958/59; 1967/68-1981/82; 1983/84; 1985/86-
　　　　HF3823.J3　GSB

Source Materials on Manchuria

MANCHURIAN GOVERNMENT PUBLICATIONS

23.1   Manchuria.
   Proclamations, statements and communications of the Manchoukuo government.   Hsinking, Manchuria, 1932.

   951.8.M268p Ser.1 STK

23.12 Manchuria. Dept. of Foreign Affairs.
   Information bulletin. no. 1- ; September 19, 1932- . Hsinking, Manchuria, 1933- .

   LIBRARY HAS: no.1-120, 1932-34
   951.8.M268pi STK

23.14 Manchuria. Dept. of Finance and Commerce.
   Annual returns of the foreign trade of Manchoukuo. 1932- . [Hsinking, Manchuria].

   Issued 1932-35 by the dept. under its earlier name, Dept. of Finance.
   Japanese and English.

   LIBRARY HAS: 1932-34; 1935:1; 1936:1; 1937:1-2; 1938:1-2
   382.518.M269 STK

23.16 Manchuria. Dept. of Foreign Affairs.
   Publications of the Dept. of Foreign Affairs, Manchoukuo Government. Combined ed.   Hsinking, Manchuria, 1933.

   Contents: Series no. 1. Proclamations, statements, and communications of the Manchoukuo government.--Series no. 2. The Chief Executive proclamation, the organic law of Manchoukuo and other laws governing various government offices.--Series no. 3. The Central Bank of Manchou and laws relating thereto with appendix.--Series no. 4. Manchoukuo and the League of Nations.

   DS784.A43 HOV

23.18 Manchuria. Dept. of Finance and Commerce.
   Monthly returns of the foreign trade of Manchoukuo.
   Jan. 1933- .   [Hsinking, Manchuria].

   Japanese and English.

   LIBRARY HAS: 1933-38
   382.518.M268 STK

23.2   Manchuria. Dept. of Foreign Affairs.
    General survey of conditions of Manchoukuo, with special emphasis on economic developments. [1934]-   . Hsinking, Manchuria, 1934-   .

    Prepared by the Department of Foreign Affairs, Manchoukuo Government.

        LIBRARY HAS: 1935-36
        915.18.M268g   STK

23.22   Manchuria. Treaties, etc., 1932-   (Pu I).
    Records of treaties, conventions, etc. between Manchoukuo and foreign states.   Hsinking, Manchuria : Foreign Office, 1941-   .

        LIBRARY HAS: v.1, 1941
        DS784.A6   HOV

JAPANESE SOURCES

24.1   South Manchuria Railway Company.
    Report on progress in Manchuria. [1st]-   ; 1907/28-   . Dairen, 1929-   .

        LIBRARY HAS: no.1-6, 1907/28-1939
        HE3289.M3S72   STK

24.12   Manchoukuo year book. 1931-   .   Hsinking, Manchuria [etc.]

    Issued 1931-   by Toa-keizai Chosakyoku (East-Asiatic Economic Investigation Bureau).
    Title varies: 1931-1932/33, Manchuria year book.
    Vols. for 1934-   include section, "Who's who in Manchoukuo."

        LIBRARY HAS: 1931-34; 1942
        315.18.M318   STK

24.14   Sino-Japanese entanglements, 1931-1932 (a military record).
    Tokyo : The Herald Press, [1932].

    "Material from official sources bearing upon the military operations in Manchuria and about Shanghai ... " -- Foreword.

        951.8.S617   STK

24.16   Japan. Foreign Office.
           Relations of Japan with Manchuria and Mongolia.
        [n.p.], 1932.

           "Document prepared by the Japanese government and communicated to the Commission of Enquiry appointed by the Council of the League of Nations in pursuance of its resolution of December 10, 1931."

              952.5.J35 Doc.B   STK

24.18   Japan.
           Appeal by the Chinese government. Observations of the Japanese government on the report of the Commission of Enquiry.
        [Geneva, 1932].

              951.8.L434o   STK

24.2   Japan. Delegation to the League of Nations.
           The Manchurian question; Japan's case in the Sino-Japanese dispute as presented before the League of Nations.
        Geneva : Japanese Delegation to the League of Nations, 1933.

           "Observations of the Japanese government on the Report of the Commission of Enquiry, memorandum of the Japanese delegation, and addresses delivered by Yosuke Matsuoka, chief delegate ..."

              951.8.J33   STK

24.22   Japan. Delegation to the League of Nations.
           Japan's case in the Sino-Japanese dispute as presented before the Special Session of the Assembly of the League of Nations.
        Geneva : Japanese Delegation to the League of Nations, 1933.

              951.8.J33ja   STK

24.24   Sakatani, Kiichi.
           Banditry, a menace in the past (restoration of peace and order in Manchoukuo) / by Kiichi Sakatani.   [Dairen : Printed by the Manchuria Daily News, 1933].

              915.18.S158   STK

24.26   Contemporary Manchuria; a bi-monthly magazine.   v. 1-5;
           Apr. 1937-Jan. 1941.   Dairen : The South Manchuria Railway Co., [1937]-   .

              LIBRARY HAS: 1-5, 1937-41//
              330.9518.C761   STK

BRITISH AND U.S. GOVERNMENT SOURCES

25.1   U.S. Consulate, Newchang, China.
           Despatches from United States consuls in Newchang, 1865-1906.
        Washington : National Archives, 1947.
           7 reels.

              MFILM N.S. 709   MTXT

25.12   Great Britain. Foreign Office.
           Correspondence respecting the Russian occupation of Manchuria
        and Newchang.   London : Printed for HMSO by Harrison and Sons,
        1904.

              DS740.5.R8G78   HOV   Sokolsky Coll.

25.14   U.S. Consulate, Mukden, Manchuria.
           Despatches from United States consuls in Mukden, 1904-1906.
        Washington : National Archives, National Archives and Records
        Service, General Services Administration, 1957.
           1 reel.

              MFILM N.S. 699   MTXT

25.16   Great Britain. Foreign Office. Historical Section.
           Manchuria.   London : HMSO, 1920.

              940.008.G786 v.12   STK

MISCELLANEOUS SOURCES

26.1   Carnegie Endowment for International Peace. Division of
           International Law.
           Manchuria, treaties and agreements.   Washington : The
        Endowment, 1921.

           "The documents have been selected chiefly from John V. A.
        MacMurray's Treaties and agreements with and concerning China."

              341.6.C280p no.44   STK

26.12   Manchurian month. no.1-152, Oct. 1, 1922-June 1, 1936.
        Dairen, 1922-36.

        Title varies: Oct. 1, 1922-Nov. 1, 1933, Manchuria daily news. Monthly supplement.
        Absorbed: Light of Manchuria.
        Superseded by: Manchuria; semi-monthly publication of the Manchuria daily news.

            LIBRARY HAS: no.1-12; no.14-41; no.43-152//
            951.8005.M268   STK

26.14   China.
        Le conflit sino-japonais. Memoranda du gouvernement chinois presentes a la Commission d'Etudes de la Societe des Nations. Nanking et Peiping, avril-aout 1932.

            DS783.7.L434C4   HOV

26.16   Hsu, Tun-chang, ed.
        Secret documents relating to the Japanese policy toward Manchuria and Mongolia / edited by Tun-chang Hsu.
        Peiping : [China Institute of International Affairs], 1932.

            DS845.H873   HOV

26.18   League of Nations. Commission of Enquiry into the Manchurian Question.
        Appeal by the Chinese government. Report of the Commission of Enquiry...signed by the members of the Commission on September 4th, 1932, at Peiping.   [Geneva, 1932].

            951.8.L996   STK

26.2   League of Nations. Special Assembly, 1932- .
        The verdict of the League; China and Japan in Manchuria; the official documents with notes and an introduction by Manley O. Hudson.   Boston : World Peace Foundation, 1933.

        "List of the principal official documents": p. [101]-102.

            951.8.L434v   STK

26.22   Manchuria; semi-monthly publication of the Manchuria Daily
        News. v.1-   ; July 1, 1936- .
        Dairen, [1936-].

        Supersedes: Manchuria daily news. Monthly supplement.
        Subtitle varies.

            LIBRARY HAS: 1-5, 1936-40
            915.1805.M268   STK

26.24   Manchoukuo.
        Hsinking, Manchoukuo, [19 -].

        Issues for 19   published by the Manchuria Daily News.

            LIBRARY HAS: 1941
            DS784.M266   HOV

Source Materials on Korea and the Korean War

KOREAN GOVERNMENT SOURCES

27.1 Korea. Treaties, etc.
    Treaties, regulations, etc., between Corea and other powers, 1876-1889. Published by order of the Inspector General of Customs. Shanghai : Statistical Department of the Inspectorate General of Customs ; London : P. S. King & Son, 1891.

    341.2519.K84t STK

27.12 Korea. Legation (U.S.).
    Notes from the Korean Legation in the United States to the Dept. of State, Sept. 18, 1883-Apr. 24, 1906. Washington : National Archives, 1949.
    1 reel.

    MFILM N.S. 1256 MTXT

27.14 Korea.
    Report on the foreign trade. 1885- . [Tokyo, etc.].

    Published 1885- by China. Inspectorate General of Customs; , by Japan. Bureau of Customs.
    Title varies: 1885, Annual reports on the trade in foreign vessels.

    LIBRARY HAS: 1885; 1911-12
    382.519.K84 STK

27.16 Korea. Ministry of Justice.
    Translation of official report [made by a vice-minister of justice to Yi Pom Chin, minister of law] concerning the attack on the Royal Palace at Seoul, Korea, and the murder of Her Majesty, the Queen, on October 8th, 1895. Seoul : Trilingual Press, [1896].

    DS915.A32 HOV

27.18　Korea (Government-General of Chosen, 1910-1945).
　　　Report on administration of Chosen. 1907-   .
　　Keijo [etc.].

　　　Compiled 1907-1908/09 by His Imperial Japanese Majesty's Residency General; 1909/10-   , by the Government-General of Chosen.
　　　Title varies: 1907-1909/10, Report on reforms and progress in Korea; 1910/11-1918/21, Report on reforms and progress in Chosen (Korea).

　　　　GREEN HAS: 1907-1932/33; 1934/35-1935/36; 1937/38
　　　　915.19.K84   STK

　　　　HOOVER HAS: 1924-38
　　　　G.D. KOREA   HOV

27.2　Korea. Treaties, etc.
　　　Korean treaties / compiled by Henry Chung. New York : H. S. Nichols, 1919.

　　　　341.2519.K84   STK

27.22　Korean reports; reports from the cabinet ministries of the
　　　　Republic of Korea. v.[1]-6; 1948/52-1958. Washington.
　　　6 v.

　　　Vols. for 1948/52-1955 issued by the Washington Bureau of the Korean Pacific Press; 1957-58, by the Korean Research and Information Office.
　　　Vols. for 1952/53-1955 prepared by the Office of Public Information of the Republic of Korea.

　　　　DS917.A32   STK

27.24　Korea (Republic). Army. Office of Information.
　　　　Republic of Korea Army. v.1-   . [Seoul], 1954-   .

　　　　LIBRARY HAS: 1954; 1957-58
　　　　US852.A2   HOV

U.S. GOVERNMENT SOURCES ON RELATIONS WITH KOREA

28.1　U.S. Dept. of State.
　　　Diplomatic instructions of the Department of State, 1801-1906. Washington : National Archives, 1945-46.

　　　Partial contents: Reel 109, Korea.

　　　　MFILM N.S. 908   MTXT

28.12 U.S. Dept. of State.
    Notes to foreign legations in the United States from the Department of State, 1834-1906. Washington : National Archives, 1947.

    Partial contents: Reel 68, Korea, Persia, and Siam.

        MFILM N.S. 1253 MTXT

28.14 U.S. Dept. of State.
    Despatches from United States ministers to Korea, 1883-1905. Washington : National Archives, National Archives and Records Service, General Services Administration, 1951.
    22 reels.

    Arranged chronologically; first reel includes calendar.

        MFILM N.S. 1253 MTXT

28.16 U.S. Consulate, Seoul, Korea.
    Despatches from United States consuls in Seoul, 1886-1906. Washington : National Archives, 1949.
    2 reels.

    "Register, 1886-1906": reel 1.
    Contents: v.1. July 3, 1886-Dec. 21, 1898;--v.2. Jan. 19, 1899-July 5, 1906.

        MFILM N.S. 4017 MTXT

28.18 U.S. Embassy. Korea.
    United States agreements with the Republic of Korea, collected for the convenience and use of the agencies of the United States government. [Tokyo : Army AG Admin. Cen.], 1954.

        327.73519.U58 STK

MISCELLANEOUS U.S. GOVERNMENT SOURCES

29.1 U.S. Congress. Senate. Committee on Foreign Relations.
    The United States and the Korean problem: Documents, 1943-1953. Washington : U.S. GPO, 1953.

    "Presented by Mr. [A.] Wiley."

        DS917.U584 HOV

29.12   U.S. Dept. of State. Office of Public Affairs.
        Korea, 1945-1948. A report on political developments and economic resources with selected documents. [Washington : U.S. GPO, 1948].

        DS916.U589   HOV

29.14   Korea (Territory under U.S. Occupation, 1945-1948). Office of Administration. Statistical Research Division.
        History of the United States Army Military Government in Korea: Period of September 1945 - 30 June 1946.
        1 reel.

        MFILM N.S. 2676   MTXT

29.16   Korea (Territory under U.S. Occupation, 1945-1948). Military Governor.
        Report. no. 1- . [Seoul, 1947-].

        LIBRARY HAS: no.1-4, 1947-48
        Call no. varies -- consult Hoover public catalog.

29.18   Korea (South Korean Interim Government). National Economic Board.
        South Korean Interim Government activities, United States Army Military Government in Korea. no. 6-35; Mar. 1946-Oct. 1948.

        Continues: Supreme Commander for the Allied Powers. Summation...non-military activities in Japan and Korea.
        Title varies: no. 1-22, Mar. 1946-July 1947, Summation... United States Army Military Government activities in Korea; no.35- , Economic summation.
        No. 35-   prepared by Korea (Republic). Civil Affairs Section.
        Issue for August 1947 called no. 1. No. 23 omitted in numbering.

        D802.K8U58   STK

KOREAN WAR: ORIGINS AND SETTLEMENT

30.1   Korea (Democratic People's Republic). Ministry of Foreign Affairs.
        Documents and materials exposing the instigators of the civil war in Korea; documents from the archives of the Rhee Syngman government. Pyongyang, 1950.

        DS910.2.U6K8   HOV

30.12 The Soviet Union and American intervention in Korea
       (documents). [Moscow, 1950].
       3 v. in 1.

   Chiefly reprints from Pravda and Izvestiia.

       DS918.S729   HOV

30.14 U.S. Congress. Senate. Committee on Armed Services.
       Military situation in the Far East. Hearings...to conduct an
   inquiry into the military situation in the Far East and the
   facts surrounding the relief of General of the Army MacArthur
   from his assignments in that area.
       5 pts.

       DS918.U582   HOV

30.16 U.S. Congress. Senate. Committee on Armed Services.
       Compilation of certain published information on the military
   situation in the Far East. Washington : U.S. GPO, 1951.

       DS918.U581   HOV

30.18 Declassified transcript of the hearings held in joint session
       by the Armed Services Committee and the Foreign Relations
       Committee from April 30, 1951, to August 17, 1951, on the
       military situation in the Far East and on the dismissal of
       General Douglas MacArthur from his command in that area.
       Washington : National Archives and Records Services, General
       Services Administration, 1976.
       8 reels.

   Project also called: MacArthur hearings, 1951.

       MFILM N.S. 3002   MTXT

30.2 Great Britain. Foreign Office.
       Further summary of events relating to Korea, October 1950 to
   May 1951, with annexes. London : HMSO, 1951.

       Brit.Doc. 1950-51 v.33   GOV

30.22 Documents on the cease-fire and armistice negotiations in
       Korea. [Peking] : People's China, [1951].
       3 v. in 2.

       DS918.D637   HOV

30.24 Chung-kuo jen min pao wei shih chieh ho p'ing wei yuan hui.
Documents and materials on the Korean armistice negotiations, with special reference to item 4 of the agenda dealing with the question of prisoners of war. Peking : Chinese People's Committee for World Peace, 1952- .

    LIBRARY HAS: v.1-2
    DS921.7.C559 HOV

30.26 United Nations Command.
[Korean Military Conference Armistice documents. Panmunjon, 1951-53].
57 folders in 10 boxes.

    (V) DS921.7.U57 W.H. Vatcher, Jr. Collection HOV

30.28 Great Britain. Foreign Office.
Korea; a summary of developments in the armistice negotiations and the prisoner of war camps, June 1951-May 1952. London : HMSO, 1952.

    Brit.Doc. 1951-52 v.31 GOV

30.3 Great Britain. Foreign Office.
Korea; a summary of further developments in the military situation, armistice negotiations, and prisoner of war camps up to January 1953. London : HMSO, [1953]

    Brit.Doc. 1952-53 v.30 GOV

30.32 United Nations Command.
Armistice agreement [signed at Panmunjom, Korea, July 27, 1953; and Temporary agreement supplementary to the Armistice agreement. n.p., 1953].
2 v.

    DS921.7.A22 HOV

30.34 United Nations Command.
Special report of the Unified Command on the Korean armistice agreement signed at Panmunjom on July 27, 1953. London : HMSO, 1953.

Includes armistice agreement.

    Brit.Doc. 1952-53 v.30 GOV

30.36　Geneva. Conference, 1954.
　　　The 1954 Geneva Conference; Indo-China and Korea.
　　New York : Greenwood Press, [1968].

　　　"Combining Documents relating to the discussion of Korea and
　　Indo-China at the Geneva Conference, April 27-June 15, 1954,
　　and Further documents relating to the discussion of Indo-China
　　at the Geneva Conference, June 17-July 21, 1954."

　　　　DS921.7.G5 1954ab　STK

KOREAN WAR: MILITARY OPERATIONS

31.1　Korean conflict: A collection of historical manuscripts on the
　　　Korean campaign held by the U.S. Army Center of Military
　　　History. [n.p., 195-　].
　　　9 reels.

　　　Consists of 39 reports, most of which were written by the
　　Military History Section of the Eighth U.S. Army Korea,
　　describing army participation in various operations, battles,
　　and campaigns during the Korean War.

　　　　MFILM DS918.K85　HOV

31.12　United States.
　　　United Nations action in Korea under unified command; report
　　to the Security Council. 1st- ; July 25, 1950- .

　　　Title varies: 1st, Action in Korea under unified command.

　　　　LIBRARY HAS: no.1-9
　　　　JX1977.A1U61 v.54-56, 59-60, 62-63, 65-66　HOV

31.14　U.S. Dept. of the Army. Office of Military History.
　　　United States Army in the Korean Conflict / by Paul C.
　　McGrath, Dept. of the Army, Office of the Chief of Military
　　History. Washington : Library of Congress, Photoduplication
　　Service, [1977].
　　　1 reel.

　　　　MFILM N.S. 2675　MTXT

31.16   U.S. Marine Corps.
U.S. Marine operations in Korea, 1950-1953. Washington : Historical Branch, G-3, Headquarters, U.S. Marine Corps, 1954 [i.e. 1955]- .

Partial contents: v.1. The Pusan perimeter / by L. Montross and N. A. Canzona.--v.3. The Chosin Reservoir campaign / by L. Montross and N. A. Canzona.--v.5. Operations in West Korea / by P. Meid and J. M. Yingling.

LIBRARY HAS: v.1; v.3; v. 5
DS919.A516   HOV

31.18   Field, James A.
History of United States naval operations: Korea. Washington : [U.S. GPO], 1962.

DS920.A2F5   STK

31.2   United Nations Command.
Civil assistance and economic affairs: Korea. 1950/51- . [n.p.]

Reports for 1953/54-   prepared by the Korea Civil Assistance Command.
Title varies: 1950/51, Civilian relief and economic aid: Korea.

951.94.U59   HOV

KOREAN WAR: PRISONERS OF WAR

32.1   U.S. Army. Pacific Division. Office of the Assistant Chief of Staff, G-3. Military History Office.
The handling of prisoners of war during the Korean War. Washington : Library of Congress, Photoduplication Service, [1977].
1 reel.

MFILM N.S. 2677   MTXT

32.12   U.S. Army. Forces in the Far East.
    Logistical support to prisoners of war, July 1951-July 1953 / prepared by the Military History Section, Headquarters, Army Forces Far East. [Seoul?, 1955?].
    1 reel.

    From the Historical Manuscripts File, Office of the Chief of Military History.

        MFILM DS921.U5   HOV

32.14   Great Britain. Ministry of Defence.
    Treatment of British prisoners of war in Korea.   London : HMSO, 1955.

        DS921.G7 1955   STK

32.16   U.S. Congress. House. Committee on Un-American Activities.
    Investigation of communist propaganda among prisoners of war in Korea, Save Our Sons Committee. Hearings...June 18 and 19, 1956. Washington : U.S. GPO, 1956.

        E743.5.E729 1956 v.2 Steel Collection   HOV

32.18   U.S. Army. Forces in the Far East.
    Operation Little Switch / prepared by the Military History Section, Headquarters, Army Forces Far East.   Seoul, 1953.
    4 v. on 2 reels.

    From the Historical Manuscripts File, Office of the Chief of Military History.
    Contents: v.1. Base camp - P´anmunjom operations and public information activities.--v.2. Medical processing and evacuation of repatriated prisoners.--v.3. Korean Communications Zone repatriation operation.--v.4. Logistical support.

        MFILM DS921.2.U5   HOV

MISCELLANEOUS SOURCES

33.1   K´uei-ling.
    Journal d´une mission en Coree, par Koei-ling, ambassadeur de S. M. l´empereur de la Chine pres la cour de Coree en 1866. Traduit du chinois par F. Scherzer.   Paris : E. Lerous, 1877.

    K´uei-ling was the last Chinese envoy to Korea to receive acknowledgement of China´s suzerainty.

        DS740.5.K8K95   HOV

33.12 McCune, George McAfee, ed.
Korean-American relations: Documents pertaining to the Far Eastern diplomacy of the United States / edited, with an introduction, by George M. McCune and John A. Harrison. Berkeley : University of California Press, 1951-63.

Contents: v.1. The initial period, 1883-1886.--v.2. The period of growing influence, 1887-1895. Edited with an introduction by Spencer J. Palmer.

    LIBRARY HAS: v.1-2
    327.73519.M133 STK

33.13 Anglo-American and Chinese diplomatic materials relating to Korea, 1887-1897 / edited by Park Il-keun. Pusan Chikhalsi : Institute of Chinese Studies, Pusan National University, 1984.

    JX633.A82 1984 STK

33.14 Rockhill, William Woodville, ed.
Treaties and conventions with or concerning China and Korea, 1894-1904, together with various state papers and documents affecting foreign interests. Washington : U.S. GPO, 1904.

    JX926.R682 HOV

33.16 Satow, Sir Ernest Mason.
Korea and Manchuria between Russia and Japan, 1895-1904; the observations of Sir Ernest Satow, British Minister Plenipotentiary to Japan (1895-1900) and China (1900-1906) / selected and edited, with a historical introduction, by George Alexander Lensen. Tallahassee : Diplomatic Press, [1966].

    DS515.S253 HOV

33.18 Rockhill, William Woodville, comp.
Treaties, conventions, agreements, ordinances, etc. relating to China and Korea (October 1904-January 1908), being a supplement to Rockhill's Treaties and conventions with or concerning China and Korea, 1894-1904. Washington : U.S. GPO, 1908.

    JX926.R683 HOV

33.2   Japan. Residency General, Seoul, Korea.
        Recent progress in Korea. [London and Tonbridge : Bradbury,
        Agnew & Co., 1910?].

            915.19.J35   STK

33.22   La Coree libre; revue mensuelle, politique, economique et
            litteraire. t. 1- ; mai 1920- .
            Paris : [Imp. des Arts et des Sports].

            LIBRARY HAS: v.1-2, no.9/13 (May 1920-May 1921)
            D643.A7.DP6K8C797   HOV

33.24   Carnegie Endowment for International Peace. Division of
            International Law.
            Korea: treaties and agreements.   Washington : The Endowment,
        1921.

            341.6.C280p no.43   STK

33.26   Materials on Korean communism, 1945-1947 / translated and
            edited by Chong-sik Lee. Honolulu : Center for Korean
            Studies, University of Hawaii, c1977.

            HX415.5.A6M37   HOV

33.28   Bank of Korea.
            Monthly statistical review. v. 1-23, no. 3; May 1947-Mar.
            1969.   [Seoul].

            Issued   -Feb. 1948 by the bank under its earlier name:
        Chosun Bank.
            Title varies: Dec. 1948-Sept. 1949, Monthly economic
        statistics.

            LIBRARY HAS: [1948-71]
            332.15.B2185m   STK

Miscellaneous Source Materials on East Asia

SOUTHEAST ASIA AND THE VIETNAM WAR

34.1 CIA research reports: Vietnam and Southeast Asia, 1946-1976.
Frederick, Md. : University Publications of America, c1982.
7 reels.

    MFILM N.S. 3830 MTXT

34.102 Lester, Robert.
Vietnam and Southeast Asia, 1946-1976: [Guide]. Frederick, Md. : University Publications of America, c1983.

    DS550.L4 1984 MTXT & GOV

34.12 U.S armed forces in Vietnam, 1954-1975. Frederick, Md. : University Publications of America, 1983.
21 reels.

Contents: Pt. 1. Indochina studies (4 reels).--pt. 2. Vietnam: Lessons learned (8 reels).--pt. 3. Vietnam: reports of U.S. Army operations (5 reels).--pt. 4. Vietnam: U.S. Army senior officer debriefing reports (4 reels).

    MFILM N.S. 3848 MTXT

34.122 McClure, Ruth.
U.S. armed forces in Vietnam, [1954-1975]: [Guide]. Frederick, Md. : University Publications of America, c1983.
4 v.

    DS558.5.U54 1983 MTXT & GOV

34.13 Westmoreland, William Childs.
Westmoreland v. CBS. New York : Clearwater Publishing Co., 1985.
1010 microfiche.

At head of title: Vietnam, a documentary collection.

    MFICHE 722 MTXT

34.14 Vietnam and Southeast Asia: Special studies, 1960-1980.
Frederick, Md. : University Publications of America, 1982.
13 reels.

    MFILM N.S. 3041 MTXT

34.142 Kesaris, Paul.
    Vietnam and Southeast Asia, 1960-1980 / edited by Paul Kesaris; guide compiled by Robert Lester. Frederick, Md. : University Publications of America, 1982.

    DS557.A6K37 MTXT

34.16 Vietnam: National Security Council histories / [edited by Paul Kesaris; guide compiled by Joan Gibson]. Frederick, Md. : University Publications of America, [1981?].
8 reels.

    Contents: Reel 1. Presidential decisions: Gulf of Tonkin attacks of August 1964.--reels 2-3. Deployment of major U.S. forces to Vietnam: July 1965.--reel 4. Honolulu Conference: February 6-8, 1966.--reel 5. Manila Conference and President's Asian trip: October 17-November 2, 1966.--reels 6-8. President Lyndon Johnson's speech of March 31, 1968.

    MFILM N.S. 3622 MTXT

34.162 Gibson, Joan.
    A guide to The war in Vietnam: classified histories by the National Security Council. Frederick, Md. : University Publications of America, [1981?].

    DS558.G84 MTXT

34.18 Transcripts and files of the Paris peace talks on Vietnam, 1968-1973 / [edited by Paul Kesaris]. Frederick, Md. : University Publications of America, 1982.
12 reels.

    MFILM N.S. 3649 MTXT

34.182 Transcripts and files of the Paris peace talks on Vietnam, 1968-1973 / edited by Paul Kesaris; guide compiled by Kenneth D. Schlessinger. Frederick, Md. : University Publications of America, c1982.

    DS559.7.T73 MTXT

THE FAR EAST IN GENERAL

35.1   U.S. Joint Chiefs of Staff.
            Records of the Joint Chiefs of Staff: The Far East, 1946-53.
        Frederick, Md. : University Publications of America, c1979.
            14 reels and guide.

            Awaiting cataloging for MTXT

35.12   Asia: Special studies, 1980-1982. Supplement.   Frederick,
            Md. : University Publications of America, c1983.
            5 reels.

            Title on box: Asia special studies supplement, 1980-1982.

            MFILM N.S. 3816   MTXT

35.122 Asia: Special studies, 1980-1982. Supplement: [Guide] /
            edited by Robert Lester.   Frederick, Md. : University
            Publications of America, c1983.

            DS503.A8 1983   MTXT

INDEX

Action in Korea under unified command 31.12
Agricultural and commercial statistics 13.16
AGRICULTURE--CHINA 2.2, 2.22
AGRICULTURE--JAPAN 13.14, 13.16
American diplomacy in the Far East; official press
    releases of the U.S. Department of State on the
    Sino-Japanese situation 8.22
American diplomatic and public papers: The United
    States and China. Series I: The treaty system
    and the Taiping Rebellion, 1842-1860 .... 10.1
American diplomatic and public papers: The United
    States and China. Series II, the United States,
    China, and imperial rivalries 10.16
American diplomatic and public papers: The
    United States and China. Series III, the Sino-
    Japanese War to the Russo-Japanese War,
    1894-1905 .... 10.2
American Institute of Pacific Relations 17.24
AMERICAN PEACE CRUSADE 32.16
Anglo-American and Chinese diplomatic materials
    relating to Korea, 1887-1897 .... 33.13
Annual report of Shanghai commodity prices 2.32
Annual returns of the foreign trade of Manchoukuo ... 23.14
Annual trade report and returns 1.2
Annual reports on the trade in foreign vessels 27.14
Appeal by the Chinese government. Observations of
    the Japanese government on the report of the
    Commission of Enquiry 24.18
Appeal by the Chinese government. Report of the
    Commission of Enquiry 26.18
Armistice agreement signed at Panmunjom, Korea,
    July 27, 1953 .... 30.32
ASIA--ECONOMIC CONDITIONS 35.12-35.122
ASIA--FOREIGN RELATIONS--JAPAN 22.58
ASIA--FOREIGN RELATIONS--SOURCES 35.12-35.122
ASIA--FOREIGN RELATIONS--U.S. 21.2
ASIA--MILITARY POLICY 35.12-35.122
ASIA--POLITICS AND GOVERNMENT--SOURCES 21.2
ASIA, SOUTHEASTERN--BIBLIOGRAPHY 34.142
ASIA, SOUTHEASTERN--HISTORY 34.1-34.102
ASIA, SOUTHEASTERN--HISTORY--SOURCES 21.18-21.182, 34.14
ASIA, SOUTHEASTERN--SOURCES--INDEXES 34.102
Asia: Special studies, 1980-1982. Supplement 35.12-35.122
Asia special studies supplement, 1980-1982 .... 35.12-35.122
ATOMIC BOMB--HISTORY--U.S. 18.23-18.232
Banditry, a menace in the past (restoration of
    peace and order in Manchoukuo) 24.24
Bank of Korea 33.28
Beasley, William G. 22.12
Benda, Harry Hindrich 22.54

Boehm, Randolph 19.12-19.122
BOXERS 4.28, 5.14-5.16
BOXERS--INDEMNITIES 4.52, 4.56
Brief progress report on the political reorientation
    of Japan 20.2
British Foreign Office Japan correspondence,
    1856- 1905. Indexes and guides 14.102
British Foreign Office Japan correspondence,
    1856-1940 .... 14.16, 14.2
British Foreign Office Japan correspondence,
    1930-1940 .... 14.162
British Foreign Office Japan correspondence,
    1941-1945 .... 14.2-14.202
Bulletin of financial statistics 12.2
Bureau of Economic Information, Peking 2.16, 2.2, 2.22
Buxton, Sydney Charles 4.56
CBS, Inc. 34.13
CIA research reports: China, 1949-1976 .... 7.1
CIA research reports: Vietnam and Southeast
    Asia, 1946-1976 .... 34.1-34.102
Calendar to the MAGIC documents 18.102
Campbell, Charles William 4.32
Canzona, Nicholas A. 31.16
Carnegie Endowment for International Peace. Division
    of International Law 22.36, 26.1, 33.24
Centre for East Asian Cultural Studies, Tokyo ... 22.14
Center of Military History 31.1
Ch'en, Ho-hsien 22.16
China [author] 17.12, 26.14
CHINA--ADDRESSES, ESSAYS, LECTURES 10.44
China and Far East finance and commerce 10.3
China and India 9.14
China and India: 1950-1969 supplement 9.145
China and Japan in Manchuria 26.2
China. Bureau of Foreign Trade 2.16, 2.22
China. Bureau of Industrial and Economic Infor-
    mation 2.16
China. Bureau of Markets 2.18, 2.24
CHINA--COMMERCE 1.1-1.3, 5.12, 7.12
CHINA--COMMERCE--GREAT BRITAIN 5.14-5.16
CHINA--COMMERCE--PERIODICALS 9.12, 10.3
China correspondence 4.12
CHINA--ECONOMIC CONDITIONS 2.16, 2.2-2.22,
                                                  5.12-5.16, 7.1-7.12,
                                                  8.2-8.212, 8.28-8.282,
                                                  9.12
CHINA--ECONOMIC POLICY 18.18, 9.145
CHINA--ECONOMIC RELATIONS--GREAT BRITAIN 5.14-5.16
CHINA--FOREIGN RELATIONS 2.3, 4.44, 8.14,
                                                  33.14, 33.18
CHINA--FOREIGN RELATIONS--1900-1903 .... 10.22
CHINA--FOREIGN RELATIONS--1930-1949 .... 8.2-8.212, 8.28-8.282
CHINA--FOREIGN RELATIONS--1950-1969 .... 9.145
CHINA--FOREIGN RELATIONS--FRANCE 10.18

CHINA--FOREIGN RELATIONS--GREAT BRITAIN	4.1-4.182, 4.26-4.28, 4.34, 5.14-5.16
CHINA--FOREIGN RELATIONS--INDIA	10.4
CHINA--FOREIGN RELATIONS--JAPAN	2.12, 8.22, 17.12, 22.16, 22.34-22.36, 22.4-22.44, 24.14, 24.18-24.22, 26.14, 26.18-26.2
CHINA--FOREIGN RELATIONS--KOREA	33.1, 33.13
CHINA--FOREIGN RELATIONS--RUSSIA	10.24, 25.12
CHINA--FOREIGN RELATIONS--TREATIES	1.28, 21.1, 26.1
CHINA--FOREIGN RELATIONS--U.S.	2.1, 6.1-6.18, 6.22-6.24, 6.28-6.5, 8.12, 8.16, 8.22-8.26, 9.115, 9.14, 10.12-10.14, 10.28, 17.12, 25.1, 25.14
CHINA--FOREIGN RELATIONS--U.S.--SOURCES	8.215-8.2152, 9.11, 10.1, 10.16, 10.2
CHINA--FOREIGN TRADE	1.22, 5.14-5.16
China. Hai kuan tsung shui wu ssu shu	1.1-1.3, 27.1, 27.14
China handbook	10.36
CHINA--HISTORY--1900-1939	4.28, 8.12-8.124, 10.24, 10.34, 13.18
CHINA--HISTORY--1946-1979	7.1-7.102, 9.145, 10.38, 10.42
CHINA--HISTORY--1949-1976	7.1
CHINA--HISTORY--BOXER REBELLION, 1899-1901	4.26
CHINA--HISTORY--KUANG-HSU, 1875-1908--SOURCES	10.2
CHINA--HISTORY--REVOLUTION, 1911-1912	4.42-4.422
CHINA--INDUSTRIES	2.2, 5.12
China. Inspectorate General of Customs	1.1-1.3, 27.1, 27.14
China, internal affairs, 1930-1939	8.2
China, internal affairs, 1940-1944	8.21-8.212
China, internal affairs, 1945-1949	8.28-8.282
China. Legation (U.S.)	2.1
China. Ministry of Finance	2.26
China. Ministry of Foreign Affairs	2.14, 2.3
China. Ministry of Information	10.36
China. National Tariff Commission	2.18, 2.24, 2.32
China, 1946-1976: [Guide]	7.102
China, 1946-1976	7.1
CHINA--PERIODICALS	10.32
CHINA--POLITICS AND GOVERNMENT--1848-1929	4.18, 4.42-4.422, 8.12-8.124, 9.11-9.115
CHINA--POLITICS AND GOVERNMENT--1930-1939	4.18, 8.2-8.202, 9.11-9.115
CHINA--POLITICS AND GOVERNMENT--1940-1949	8.21-8.2152, 8.28-8.282, 9.11-9.115
CHINA--POLITICS AND GOVERNMENT--YEARBOOKS	10.26
CHINA--POPULATION	1.26
CHINA--RELATIONS (GENERAL) WITH GREAT BRITAIN	5.14-5.16
CHINA--RELATIONS (GENERAL) WITH THE U.S.	10.28
CHINA--SOCIAL CONDITIONS	5.14-5.16
CHINA--SOCIAL CONDITIONS--1930-1949--SOURCES	8.2-8.212, 8.28-8.282

China: Special studies, 1970-1980	10.44
China. Treaties, etc.	33.14, 33.18, 33.24
China. Treaties, etc., 1915	22.36
China. Wai chiao pu	2.14, 2.3
China weekly chronicle	10.32
China year book	10.26
China yearbook	10.36
China's economy and foreign trade	9.12
Chinese economic bulletin	2.16
Chinese economic journal	2.22
Chinese economic journal and bulletin	2.22
Chinese economic monthly	2.2
Chinese General Chamber of Commerce, Shanghai	22.4
CHINESE-JAPANESE WAR, 1931-1932	2.3, 22.4
Chinese People's Committee for World Peace	30.24
Chino-Japanese negotiations	2.12
Chosin Reservoir campaign	31.16
Chosun Bank	33.28
Chung, Henry	27.2
Chung-kuo Jen Min Pao Wei Shih Chieh Ho P'ing Wei Yuan Hui	30.24
Civil assistance and economic affairs: Korea	31.2
Civilian relief and economic aid: Korea	31.2
Clyde, Paul Hibbert	10.12
Collection and disposal of the maritime and native customs revenue since the revolution of 1911	1.3
Collection of official foreign statements on Japanese peace treaty	11.22
Columbia University. East Asian Institute	4.182
Commission on Extraterritorial Jurisdiction in China	9.1
Communiques issued by the Imperial General Headquarters from December 8, 1941 to June 30, 1943	11.18
COMMUNISM--CHINA	10.24, 10.42
COMMUNISM--KOREA	33.26
COMMUNISM--U.S.	32.16
Communist China	10.42
Compilation of certain published information on the military situation in the Far East	30.16
Confidential papers relating to China and her neighbouring countries, 1840-1914	4.14
Confidential print: China, 1848-1922	4.18, 4.182
Confidential print: Japan, 1859-1937	14.12
Confidential print: Tibet and Mongolia, 1903-1923	4.3
Confidential U.S. diplomatic post records: Japan, 1914-	16.24-16.242
Confidential U.S. State Department Central Files: China, internal affairs, 1930-1939	8.2-8.202
Confidential U.S. State Department Central Files: China, internal affairs, 1940-1944	8.21-8.212
Confidential U.S. State Department Central Files: China, internal affairs, 1945-1949	8.28-8.282
Confidential U.S. State Department Central Files: Formosa, internal affairs, 1945-1949	8.3-8.302

Confidential U.S. State Department Central Files:
    Japan, internal affairs, 1945-1949 .... 17.23-17.232
Confidential U.S. State Department Central Files:
    Japan, internal affairs, 1950-1954 .... 17.26
Confidential U.S. State Department Central Files:
    United States-China relations, 1940-1949 .... 8.215-8.2152
Conflict in the Far East 10.34
Conflit sino-japonais 26.14
Contemporary Manchuria 24.26
Coree libre; revue mensuelle, politique,
    economique et litteraire 33.22
Correspondence and reports [on China], 1837-1911 .... 10.11
Correspondence and resolutions respecting events
    in Shanghai and neighbourhood, February-
    March 1932 .... 22.42
Correspondence regarding the negotiations between
    Japan and Russia (1903-1904) 11.12
Correspondence respecting the affairs of China 4.422
Correspondence respecting the cultivation of
    opium in China 4.38
Correspondence respecting the disturbances in
    China 4.28
Correspondence respecting the Russian occupation
    of Manchuria and Newchang 25.12
COURTS--CHINA 9.1
Crothers, George Edward 10.28
CUSTOMS ADMINISTRATION--CHINA 1.112-1.116, 1.119
Customs gazette 1.14
Customs papers 1.116
Davids, Jules 10.1, 10.16, 10.2
Decennial reports on the trade, navigation,
    industries, etc. of the ports open to foreign
    commerce in China and Corea 1.12
Declassified transcripts of the hearings on the
    military situation in the Far East and on the
    dismissal of Gen. Douglas MacArthur 30.18
Despatches from Sir A. Hosie, forwarding reports re-
    specting the opium question in China 3.1
Despatches from United States consuls in Amoy,
    1844-1906 .... 6.18
Despatches from United States consuls in Antung,
    1904-1906 .... 6.46
Despatches from United States consuls in Canton,
    1790-1906 .... 6.1
Despatches from United States consuls in Chefoo,
    1863-1906 .... 6.34
Despatches from United States consuls in Chinkiang,
    1865-1902 .... 6.36
Despatches from United States consuls in Chungking,
    1896-1906 .... 6.4
Despatches from United States consuls in Foochow,
    1849-1906 .... 6.24
Despatches from United States consuls in Hakodate,
    1856-1878 .... 16.16

Despatches from United States consuls in Hangchow,
    1904-1906 .... 6.48
Despatches from United States consuls in Hankow,
    1861-1906 .... 6.32
Despatches from United States consuls in Hong Kong,
    1844-1906 .... 6.2
Despatches from United States consuls in Macao,
    1849-1896 .... 6.26
Despatches from United States consuls in Mukden,
    1904-1906 .... 25.14
Despatches from United States consuls in Nagasaki,
    1860-1906 .... 16.18
Despatches from United States consuls in Nanking,
    1902-1906 .... 6.44
Despatches from United States consuls in Newchang,
    1865-1906 .... 25.1
Despatches from United States consuls in Ningpo,
    1853-1896 .... 6.28
Despatches from United States consuls in Osaka
    and Hiogo (Kobe), 1868-1906 .... 16.2
Despatches from United States consuls in Seoul,
    1886-1906 .... 28.16
Despatches from United States consuls in Shanghai,
    1847-1906 .... 6.22
Despatches from United States consuls in Swatow,
    1860-1881 .... 6.3
Despatches from United States consuls in Tamsui,
    1898-1906: register, 1898-1906, and volume 1,
    July 22, 1898-August 7, 1906 .... 6.42
Despatches from United States consuls in Tientsin,
    1868-1906 .... 6.38
Despatches from United States consuls in Yokohama,
    1897-1906 .... 16.22
Despatches from United States ministers to China,
    1843-1906 .... 6.16
Despatches from United States ministers to Japan,
    1855-1906 .... 16.14
Despatches from United States ministers to Korea,
    1883-1905 .... 28.14
Diplomatic bluebook 11.24
Diplomatic instructions of the Department of
    State, 1801-1906: China 6.12
Diplomatic instructions of the Department of
    State, 1801-1906: [Japan] 16.1
Diplomatic instructions of the Department of
    State, 1801-1906: [Korea] 28.1
Diplomatic relations between the United States
    and Japan, 1908-1924 .... 21.14
Documents and materials exposing the instigators
    of the civil war in Korea 30.1
Documents and materials on the Korean armistice
    negotiations 30.24
Documents concerning the Allied occupation and
    control of Japan 11.2

Documents diplomatiques. Chine	10.18
Documents diplomatiques. Evacuation de Shanghai	10.22
Documents on communism, nationalism, and Soviet advisers in China, 1918-1927	10.24
Documents on the cease-fire and armistice negotiations in Korea	30.22
Documents relating to the discussion of Korea and Indo-China at the Geneva Conference, April 27-June 15, 1954	30.36
Donat, Karl von, 1853-1923	22.28
EAST ASIA--COMMERCE--PERIODICALS	10.3
EAST ASIA--ECONOMIC CONDITIONS--PERIODICALS	10.3
EAST ASIA--FOREIGN RELATIONS--U.S.	35.1
EAST ASIA--MILITARY RELATIONS--U.S.	21.16
EAST ASIA--YEARBOOKS	22.52
East-Asiatic Economic Investigation Bureau	24.12
EAST TURKESTAN--COMMERCE	5.12
EASTERN QUESTION (FAR EAST)	4.14, 8.22, 11.12, 17.1-17.12, 24.14, 25.12, 26.1, 30.16, 33.14-33.18, 33.22
Economic and commercial conditions in Japan	15.14
Economic conditions in China	5.12
Economic summary	29.18
Economic survey of Japan	12.18
EDUCATION--CHINA--SHANGHAI	4.52
Embassy and consular archives, China correspondence, 1834-1894	4.12
Embassy and consular archives, China, Shanghai, Boxer indemnity: Re-allocation to Chinese education development, 1923-1938	4.52
Embassy and consular archives, China, Shanghai supreme court, various cases, 1884-1891	4.24
Embassy and consular archives, China, Shanghai supreme court, Yunnan opium case, 1916	4.4
End of the war in the Pacific. Surrender documents in facsimile	18.22
EUROPEAN WAR, 1914-1918--CHINA	2.14
Evacuation de Shanghai	10.22
EXTRATERRITORIALITY	8.18, 9.1
Extraterritoriality in China	8.18
Far East, 1946-53	35.1
Federal records of World War II	18.14
Field, James A.	31.18
Finance and commerce	10.3
FINANCE--CHINA	2.26
FINANCE--JAPAN	12.1, 12.2, 12.26, 15.12
Financial and economical annual [of Japan]	12.1
Financial and economic annual of Japan	12.1
Foreign Affairs Association of Japan	22.46, 22.5
Foreign Office confidential papers relating to China and her neighbouring countries, 1840-1914	4.14
Foreign relations of the United States; diplomatic papers, 1942-[1949] China	8.24

Foreign trade of China	1.18
Foreign trade of Japan	12.16
FORMOSA	3.14, 8.3-8.302, 10.36
Formosa, internal affairs, 1945-1949	8.3-8.302
FRANCE--FOREIGN RELATIONS--CHINA	10.18
France. Ministere des Affaires Etrangeres	10.18, 10.22
Further correspondence respecting the affairs of China	4.422
Further documents relating to the discussion of Indo-China at the Geneva Conference, June 16-July 21, 1954	30.36
Further summary of events relating to Korea, October 1950 to May 1951	30.2
General correspondence: China, 1815-1905	4.1
General correspondence: Japan, 1856-1905	14.1
General correspondence. Political: China, 1906-	4.34
General correspondence. Political: Japan, 1906-	14.18
General report on the commercial, industrial and economic situation of China	5.12
General survey of conditions in Manchoukuo, with special emphasis on economic developments	23.2
General survey of the Japanese economy	12.26
Geneva. Conference, 1954	30.36
German official account of the Russo-Japanese War	22.28
Gibson, Joan	34.16-34.162
Great Britain. Board of Trade	15.14
Great Britain. Consulate, Peking.	3.1-3.12
Great Britain. Consulate, Tamsui, Formosa	3.14
Great Britain. Dept. of Overseas Trade	5.12, 15.12
Great Britain. Foreign Office	4.1-4.56, 14.1-14.202, 17.12, 25.12, 30.2, 30.28-30.3
Great Britain. Foreign Office. Historical Section	4.44-4.5, 14.14, 25.16
GREAT BRITAIN--FOREIGN RELATIONS	4.16, 10.18
GREAT BRITAIN--FOREIGN RELATIONS--20TH CENTURY	14.16-14.18
GREAT BRITAIN--FOREIGN RELATIONS--CHINA	4.1-4.16, 4.26-4.28, 4.34, 5.14-5.16
GREAT BRITAIN--FOREIGN RELATIONS--EAST ASIA	4.35
GREAT BRITAIN--FOREIGN RELATIONS--JAPAN	4.104, 14.1-14.102, 14.16-14.162, 14.18-14.202
GREAT BRITAIN--FOREIGN RELATIONS--KOREA	4.104, 33.13
GREAT BRITAIN--FOREIGN RELATIONS--MONGOLIA	4.3
GREAT BRITAIN--FOREIGN RELATIONS--TIBET	4.3
GREAT BRITAIN--FOREIGN RELATIONS--TREATIES	4.16
Great Britain. Ministry of Defence	32.14
Great Britain. Parliament. House of Commons	5.14
Great Britain. Parliament. House of Lords	5.16
Great Britain. Public Record Office	4.1-4.56, 14.1-14.202
Great Britain. War Office	15.1
Great Britain. War Office. General Staff	5.1
Gubbins, John Harington	14.14
Guide to Confidential U.S. State Department Central Files: Formosa, internal affairs, 1945-1949	8.302

Guide to British Foreign Office: Confidential print: China, 1848-1922	4.182
Guide to Manhattan Project: Official history and documents	18.232
Guide to records of the U.S. Department of State relating to the internal affairs of Japan, 1930-1939 and 1940-1944	17.182
Guide to the Scholarly Resources microfilm edition of Military intelligence in the Pacific, 1942-46	18.197
Guide to The war in Vietnam	34.162
Handling of prisoners of war during the Korean War	32.1
Harada, Kumao	22.185
Harrison, John A.	33.12
Hinton, Harold C.	10.38
History of the United States Army Military Government in Korea: Period of Sept. 1945-30 June 1946	29.14
History of United States naval operations: Korea	31.18
HONG KONG--FOREIGN RELATIONS--U.S.	6.2
Hosie, Alexander	3.1, 3.14
Hsia, Lien-yin	10.24
Hsin kuan ti ming lu	1.114
Hsu, Tun-chan	26.16
Hudson, Manley Ottmer	26.2
Hussey, Alfred Rodman	22.56
Hussey papers, 1945-1948	22.56
Imperial Maritime Customs. I, Special series	1.119
Imperial Maritime Customs. III, Miscellaneous series	1.112
Imperial Maritime Customs. IV, Service series	1.114
Imperial Maritime Customs. V, Office series. Customs papers	1.116
Inahara, Katsuji	22.46
INDEX NUMBERS (ECONOMICS)	2.24
INDIA	9.14-9.145
INDIA--FOREIGN RELATIONS--CHINA	10.4
India (Republic) Ministry of External Affairs	10.4
Indo-China and Korea	30.36
Industries of Japan	12.32
Internal affairs of China, 1910-1929	8.12-8.124
Internal affairs of Japan, 1910-1929	17.14-17.142
Internal affairs of Japan [1930-1939 and 1940-1944]	17.18-17.182
International Military Tribunal for the Far East	20.1-20.112, 22.58
Investigation of Communist propaganda among prisoners of war in Korea	32.16
Irikura, James K.	22.54
Iwado, Zenchi Tamotsu	13.18
JANIS [title]	18.2
Japan [author]	13.2, 24.18
Japan [title]	14.14
Japan; economic and commercial conditions in Japan	15.14
JAPAN--ADDRESSES, ESSAYS, LECTURES	21.22-21.222

Japan and its occupied territories during World War II	18.16
Japan and its occupied territories during World War II. [Guide]	18.162
JAPAN--BIBLIOGRAPHY	21.222
JAPAN--BIOGRAPHY	22.24, 22.52
Japan. Board of Information	11.16, 22.5
Japan. Bureau de la Statistique Generale	13.12, 13.22-13.26, 22.6
Japan. Bureau of Customs	27.14
Japan. Cabinet Statistical Bureau	13.12, 13.22-13.26, 22.6
Japan. Chamber of Commerce and Industry	22.62
Japan chronicle, weekly edition	22.2
JAPAN--COMMERCE	12.32, 13.16, 15.12, 22.18, 22.38
JAPAN--COMMERCE--DIRECTORIES	22.62
JAPAN--COMMERCE--STATISTICS--PERIODICALS	12.12, 12.3
JAPAN--COMMERCE--STATISTICS--YEARBOOKS	12.34
JAPAN--COMMERCE--U.S.	21.12
JAPAN--CONSTITUTIONAL HISTORY	22.56
Japan correspondence, 1856-1905	14.102
Japan correspondence, 1856-1940	14.16, 14.2
Japan correspondence, 1930-1940	14.162
Japan daily mail. Weekly edition	22.18
Japan. Delegation to the League of Nations	24.2-24.22
Japan. Dept. of Agriculture and Commerce	13.14-13.16
Japan. Dept. of Finance	12.1-12.12, 12.26, 12.3, 12.34
JAPAN--DESCRIPTION AND TRAVEL	10.14, 22.1
JAPAN--DIRECTORIES	22.24, 22.5
JAPAN--ECONOMIC CONDITIONS--1902-1944	12.1, 13.14, 17.14-17.142, 22.38, 22.48
JAPAN--ECONOMIC CONDITIONS--1945-	12.14, 12.18-12.28, 12.36, 15.14, 20.24, 17.23-17.232, 22.38, 22.48
Japan. Economic Counsel Board	12.14, 12.18, 12.22-12.24
Japan. Economic Planning Board	12.14, 12.18, 12.22-12.24
Japan. Economic Stabilization Board	12.14, 12.18
Japan. Export Trade Promotion Agency	12.16
Japan. Export Trade Research Organization	12.16
Japan exports & imports: commodity by country	12.3
Japan exports & imports: country by commodity	12.34
Japan. Foreign Office	11.1, 11.14, 17.1-17.12, 24.16
JAPAN--FOREIGN RELATIONS	11.16, 14.14, 26.16
JAPAN--FOREIGN RELATIONS--1853-1867	22.12
JAPAN--FOREIGN RELATIONS--20TH CENTURY	11.24, 14.18, 17.26, 18.1-18.104, 21.2
JAPAN--FOREIGN RELATIONS--ASIA	22.58
JAPAN--FOREIGN RELATIONS--CHINA	2.12, 8.22, 17.12, 22.16, 22.34-22.36, 22.4-22.44, 24.14, 24.18-24.22, 26.14, 26.18-26.2

```
JAPAN--FOREIGN RELATIONS--GREAT BRITAIN .............. 4.1-4.104, 14.1-14.12,
                                                       14.16-14.162, 14.18,
                                                       14.2-14.202
JAPAN--FOREIGN RELATIONS--MANCHURIA .................. 24.16
JAPAN--FOREIGN RELATIONS--MONGOLIA ................... 24.16
JAPAN--FOREIGN RELATIONS--RUSSIA ..................... 11.12, 33.16
JAPAN--FOREIGN RELATIONS--TREATIES ................... 11.14, 14.14, 21.1
JAPAN--FOREIGN RELATIONS--U.S. ....................... 8.22, 11.1, 16.1-17.12,
                                                       17.16, 17.2, 17.24,
                                                       18.12, 21.14
JAPAN--FOREIGN TRADE ................................. 12.16, 15.14
Japan. Gaimusho ...................................... 12.28
Japan. Gaimusho. Division of Special Records ......... 11.2
Japan. Gaimusho. Johobu .............................. 11.22-11.24
Japan. Gaimusho. Joho Bunkakyoku ..................... 11.22-11.24
JAPAN--GOVERNMENT PUBLICATIONS--ABSTRACTS ............ 12.36
JAPAN--HISTORY ....................................... 13.1
JAPAN--HISTORY--MEIJI PERIOD, 1868-1912 .............. 22.14
JAPAN--HISTORY--20TH CENTURY ......................... 17.18-17.182,
                                                       18.16-18.162
JAPAN--HISTORY--ALLIED OCCUPATION, 1945-1952 ......... 20.12, 20.14-20.16, 22.56
JAPAN--HISTORY--ALLIED OCCUPATION, 1945-1952--
    SOURCES .......................................... 11.2, 21.16,
                                                       21.18-21.182, 22.56
Japan. Imperial General Headquarters ................. 11.18
JAPAN--INDUSTRIES .................................... 12.32, 13.16,
                                                       15.12, 22.38
Japan Institute of International Affairs ............. 12.36
Japan, internal affairs, 1945-1949 ................... 17.23-17.232
Japan, internal affairs, 1950-1954 ................... 17.26
JAPAN. KAIGAN--WEAPONS SYSTEMS--HISTORY--SOURCES ..... 20.26
Japan. Keizai Kikakucho .............................. 12.14, 12.18, 12.22-12.24
Japan, Korea, and the security of Asia, 1946-1976 ... 21.2
Japan, Korea, and the security of Asia: Special
    studies, 1970-1980 ............................... 21.22
Japan, Korea, Southeast Asia, and the Far East
    generally ........................................ 21.18-21.182
Japan. Laws, statutes, etc. .......................... 13.1, 13.2, 14.14
Japan. Legation (U.S.) ............................... 11.1
Japan-Manchoukuo year book ........................... 22.52
JAPAN--MANUFACTURING--DIRECTORIES .................... 22.62
Japan. Ministry of Finance ........................... 12.1-12.12, 12.26, 12.3
                                                       12.34
Japan. Ministry of Finance. Research Division ........ 12.2
Japan. Ministry of Foreign Affairs. Division of
    Special Records .................................. 11.2
Japan. Ministry of Foreign Affairs. Public
    Information Division ............................. 11.22
Japan. Ministry of International Trade and Industry . 12.16, 22.48
Japan. Ministry of International Trade and
    Industry. Minister's Secretariat. Research
    and Statistics Dept. ............................. 12.32
Japan: 1931-1941 ..................................... 17.2
```

97

Japan. Okurasho	12.1-12.12, 12.26, 12.3, 12.34
Japan. Okurasho. Daijin Kambo. Chosabu	12.2
Japan. Okurasho. Kanzeikyoku	12.3
JAPAN--PERIODICALS	22.18-22.2, 22.5
JAPAN--POLITICS AND GOVERNMENT	13.1, 13.2, 14.14, 17.14, 17.26, 22.18
JAPAN--POLITICS AND GOVERNMENT--1913-1945	22.185
JAPAN--POLITICS AND GOVERNMENT--20TH CENTURY	17.14, 17.18-17.182, 17.23-17.232, 18.1-18.104, 20.18-20.24, 21.2, 22.56
Japan. Prime Minister's Office. Bureau of Statistics	13.12, 13.22-13.26, 22.6
Japan register of merchants, manufacturers & shippers	22.62
JAPAN--RELATIONS (GENERAL) WITH THE U.S.	17.24
Japan. Residency General, Seoul, Korea	27.18, 33.2
JAPAN--SOCIAL CONDITIONS	12.36, 17.14, 17.23-17.232
Japan. Sorifu. Tokeikyoku	13.12, 13.22-13.26, 22.6
Japan statistical yearbook	22.6
JAPAN--STATISTICS	12.32, 13.12, 13.22-13.26, 22.6
Japan. Statistics Commission	22.6
Japan. Taishikan (U.S.)	11.1
Japan times	22.26
Japan trade guide, with a comprehensive mercantile directory	22.48
Japan. Treaties, etc.	11.14, 21.14, 33.24
Japan. Treaties, etc., 1867-1912 (Mitsuhito)	21.12
Japan. Treaties, etc., 1912-1921 (Yoshihito)	22.36
Japan. Tsusho Sangyosho. Chosa Tokeibu	12.32
Japan weekly chronicle	22.2
Japan weekly mail	22.18
Japan year book	22.24, 22.46
JAPAN--YEARBOOKS	22.24, 22.46, 22.52, 22.6
JAPANESE AMERICANS--BIBLIOGRAPHY	19.1
JAPANESE AMERICANS--EVACUATION AND RELOCATION, 1942-1945	19.1-19.14
Japanese economic statistics. Bulletin	12.14
Japanese economic statistics. Bulletin. Rev. ed.	12.24
Japanese evacuation from the West Coast, 1942: Final report	19.14
Japanese foreign trade	12.16
Japanese government documents, 1867-1889	13.1
JAPANESE IN CHINA	18.18
JAPANESE IN KOREA	27.16
JAPANESE IN MANCHURIA	2.3, 18.18, 24.14, 24.18-24.22, 26.14, 26.18-26.22
Japanese military administration in Indonesia: Selected documents	22.54
Japanese peace treaty	11.22

Japanese techniques of occupation; key laws and official documents	18.18
Japan's case in the Sino-Japanese dispute	24.2-24.22
Japan's undeclared war in Shanghai	22.4
Japan's wartime legislation, 1939	13.18
Joint Army-Navy intelligence studies	18.2
Jordan, John Newell	3.12, 4.35
Jordan papers, 1910-1919	4.35
Journal d'une mission en Coree	33.1
JUSTICE, ADMINISTRATION OF--CHINA	9.1
Keenan, Joseph Berry	20.1
Kesaris, Paul	7.102, 8.2, 8.21-8.212, 8.215-8.2152, 8.28-8.282, 16.24-16.242, 18.102-18.104, 18.23-18.232, 21.182, 21.2, 34.1-34.182
KIANG-SU, CHINA	5.1
KIAO-CHOU	4.44
Kiaochow and Weihaiwei	4.44
Kinai, M.	22.26
Kishi, Koichi	22.54
Kobe chronicle	22.2
Korea [author]	27.14
Korea; a summary of developments in the armistice agreements, June 1951-May 1952	30.28
Korea; a summary of further developments in the military situation, armistice negotiations, and prisoner of war camps up to Jan. 1953	30.3
KOREA--ADDRESSES, ESSAYS, LECTURES	21.22
Korea and Manchuria between Russia and Japan, 1895-1904	33.16
KOREA--BIBLIOGRAPHY	21.222
Korea Civil Assistance Command	31.2
KOREA--COMMERCE	1.12, 27.14
Korea (Democratic People's Republic) Ministry of Foreign Affairs	30.1
KOREA--DESCRIPTION AND TRAVEL	33.1
KOREA--ECONOMIC CONDITIONS	27.18, 29.12, 29.16-29.18, 33.2, 33.28
KOREA--FOREIGN RELATIONS	21.2, 33.14, 33.18, 33.24
KOREA--FOREIGN RELATIONS--CHINA	33.1, 33.13
KOREA--FOREIGN RELATIONS--GREAT BRITAIN	4.104, 33.13
KOREA--FOREIGN RELATIONS--U.S.	27.12, 28.1-29.1, 30.1, 33.12-33.13
Korea (Government-General of Chosen, 1910-1945)	27.18
KOREA--HISTORY	21.18-21.182, 27.16, 29.1-29.14, 29.18
Korea. Legation (U.S.)	27.12
Korea. Ministry of Justice	27.16
Korea, 1945-1948	29.12
KOREA--POLITICS AND GOVERNMENT	27.18, 27.22, 29.18, 30.1, 33.2-33.22, 33.26
Korea (Republic) Army. Office of Information	27.24

Korea (Republic) Civil Affairs Section 29.18
Korea (Republic) Korean Research and Information
    Office 27.22
Korea (Republic) Office of Public Information 27.22
Korea (South Korean Interim Government). National
    Economic Board 29.18
KOREA (SOUTH)--POLITICS AND GOVERNMENT 21.2
KOREA--STATISTICS 33.28
Korea (Territory under U.S. Occupation, 1945-1948).
    Military Governor 29.14-29.16
Korea (Territory under U.S. Occupation, 1948-1948).
    Office of Administration. Statistical Research
    Division 29.14
Korea: Treaties and agreements 33.24
Korea. Treaties, etc. 27.1, 27.2, 33.14,
                                                       33.18, 33.24
Korean-American relations; documents pertaining
    to the Far Eastern diplomacy of the United
    States 33.12
Korean armistice negotiations 30.24
Korean Conflict: A collection of historical
    manuscripts 31.1
Korean Military Conference Armistice documents 30.26
Korean Pacific Press. Washington Bureau 27.22
Korean reports; reports from the cabinet ministries
    of the Republic of Korea 27.22
Korean treaties 27.2
KOREAN WAR, 1950-1953--ARMISTICES 30.24-30.28, 30.32-30.34
KOREAN WAR, 1950-1953--CAMPAIGNS AND BATTLES 31.1
KOREAN WAR, 1950-1953--CIVILIAN RELIEF 31.2
KOREAN WAR, 1950-1953--ECONOMIC ASPECTS 31.2
KOREAN WAR, 1950-1953--FOREIGN PARTICIPATION,
    AMERICAN 31.1, 31.14
KOREAN WAR, 1950-1953--NAVAL OPERATIONS 31.18
KOREAN WAR, 1950-1953--PEACE 30.36
KOREAN WAR, 1950-1953--PRISONERS AND PRISONS 30.24, 30.28, 30.32,
                                                       32.1-32.18
KOREAN WAR, 1950-1953--U.S.--MARINE CORPS 31.16
K'uei-ling 33.1
Kwon, Chai Hiung 27.16
LABOR AND LABORING CLASSES--CHINA 4.54
LAW--JAPAN 13.18
League of Nations 22.42-22.44, 24.18-24.22
League of Nations. Commission of Enquiry into the
    Manchurian Question 26.14, 26.18
League of Nations. Delegation from China 10.34
League of Nations. Special Assembly, 1932- 26.2
Lee, Chong-sik 33.26
Lensen, George Alexander 33.16
Lester, Robert 7.102, 8.202, 16.242,
                                                       19.12-19.122, 21.2,
                                                       34.102, 34.142,
                                                       35.12-35.122
Li, Kuo-ch'in 8.22

List of treaties, etc., between Great Britain and China (1842-1922)	4.16
Lo, Hui-min	4.14
Logistical support to prisoners of war, July 1951-July 1953	32.12
Lowe, Chuan-hua	22.4
Lytton, Victor Alexander George Robert	26.18
MACAO	4.46, 6.26
MacARTHUR, DOUGLAS, 1880-1964	30.14, 30.18
MacArthur hearings, 1951	30.18
McClure, Ruth	34.122
McCune, George McAfee	33.12
MacDonald, Claude M.	4.26
McGrath, Paul C.	31.14
McLaren, Walter Wallace	13.1
MAGIC documents: Summaries and transcripts of the secret diplomatic communications of Japan, 1938-1945	18.1-18.104
Manchoukuo [title]	26.24
Manchuria [author]	23.1
Manchuria [title]	25.16
Manchuria; semi-monthly publication of the Manchuria daily news	26.22
MANCHURIA--BIOGRAPHY	24.12
MANCHURIA--COMMERCE--STATISTICS	23.14, 23.18
Manchuria daily news	26.22-26.24
Manchuria daily news. Monthly supplement	26.12
Manchuria. Dept. of Finance and Commerce	23.14, 23.18
Manchuria. Dept. of Foreign Affairs	23.12, 23.16, 23.2-23.22
MANCHURIA--ECONOMIC CONDITIONS	23.2, 24.1, 24.26, 26.22
MANCHURIA--ECONOMIC POLICY	18.18
MANCHURIA--FOREIGN RELATIONS	23.1, 23.16, 23.22
MANCHURIA--FOREIGN RELATIONS--JAPAN	24.16
MANCHURIA--FOREIGN RELATIONS--TREATIES	23.22
MANCHURIA--FOREIGN RELATIONS--U.S.	25.1, 25.14
MANCHURIA--HISTORY	24.14, 24.26, 26.24
MANCHURIA--POLITICS AND GOVERNMENT	23.1
Manchuria, treaties and agreements	26.1
Manchuria. Treaties, etc., 1932- (Pu I)	23.22
Manchuria year book	24.12
Manchurian month	26.12
Manchurian question; Japan's case in the Sino-Japanese dispute	24.2
Manhattan Project: Official history and documents	18.23-18.232
Marshall, George Catlett	9.115
Marshall's mission to China, Dec.1945-Jan.1947; the report and appended documents	9.115
Materials on Korean communism, 1945-1947	33.26
Matsuoka, Yosuke	24.2-24.22
Medical reports	1.13
MEDICINE--CHINA	1.13
Meid, P.	31.16
Meiji Japan through contemporary sources	22.14

```
Memoranda du gouvernement chinois presentes a la
    Commission d'Etude de la Societe des Nations .....  26.14
MILITARY ART AND SCIENCE--JAPAN ......................  20.26
MILITARY GOVERNMENT ..................................  22.54
Military intelligence in the Pacific, 1942-1946 .....  18.195-18.197
MILITARY OCCUPATION ..................................  18.18
Military report on the province of Chiang-su (north
    of the Yang-tzu) .................................  5.1
Military situation in the Far East ..................  30.14, 30.18
MIN YI, QUEEN ........................................  27.16
MISSIONS--CHINA ......................................  10.11
Mitsubishi Economic Research Institute, Tokyo .......  22.38
Mitsubishi Goshi Kaisha. Economic Research
    Institute ........................................  22.38
MONGOLIA .............................................  4.48, 26.16
MONGOLIA--DESCRIPTION AND TRAVEL .....................  4.32, 4.48
MONGOLIA--FOREIGN RELATIONS--GREAT BRITAIN ...........  4.3
MONGOLIA--FOREIGN RELATIONS--JAPAN ...................  24.16
MONGOLIA--HISTORY ....................................  4.48
MONGOLIA--POLITICS AND GOVERNMENT ....................  4.48
Monthly circular; survey of economic conditions
    in Japan .........................................  22.38
Monthly economic report ..............................  12.22
Monthly return of the foreign trade of Japan ........  12.12
Monthly returns of the foreign trade of China .......  1.22
Monthly returns of the foreign trade of Manchoukuo ..  23.18
Monthly statistics of Japan ..........................  13.26
Montross, Lynn .......................................  31.16
Narrative of the expedition of an American squadron
    to the China Seas and Japan ......................  22.1
NAVAL ART AND SCIENCE--JAPAN .........................  20.26
Naval Historical Center (U.S.) .......................  18.195
Neutral Nations Repatriation Commission ..............  30.32
Nihon boeki geppyo: himbetsu kokubetsu ...............  12.3
Nihon boeki geppyo: kokubetsu himbetsu ...............  12.34
Nihon gaikoku boeki geppyo ...........................  12.12
Nihon Kokusai Mondai Kenkyujo, Tokyo..................  12.36
1954 Geneva Conference; Indo-China and Korea ........  30.36
Notes from the Chinese legation in the United
    States to the Department of State, 1868-1906 .....  2.1
Notes from the Japanese Legation in the United
    States to the Department of State, 1858-1906 .....  11.1
Notes from the Korean Legation in the United
    States to the Department of State, Sept. 18,
    1883-Apr. 24, 1906 ...............................  27.12
Notes, memoranda and letters exchanged and agreements
    signed between the Governments of India and
    China ............................................  10.4
Notes to foreign legations in the United States
    from the Department of State, 1834-1906:
    [China] ..........................................  8.1
Notes to foreign legations in the United States
    from the Department of State, 1834-1906:
    [Japan] ..........................................  16.12
```

Notes to foreign legations in the United States from the Department of State, 1834-1906: [Korea]	28.12
Observations of the Japanese government on the report of the Commission of Enquiry	24.18
Occupation of Japan, policy and progress	20.12
Occupied Japan; a summary	20.18
Office series. Customs papers	1.116
Official documents concerning foreign relations: [Japan]	11.16
Official documents relating to Japan's undeclared war in Shanghai	22.4
Official documents relating to the war	2.14
Official gazette. English ed.	13.2
Operation Little Switch	32.18
Operations in West Asia	31.16
OPIUM TRADE	3.1-3.12, 4.35-4.4, 5.14-5.16
Opium trade, 1910-1941	4.36
Orient year book	22.52
Pacific survey	18.2
Pacific theater, 1942-1945	18.19
Pak, Il-gun	33.13
Palmer, Spencer J.	33.12
Pamphlet accompanying Microcopy 329: Records of the Department of State relating to internal affairs of China, 1910-1929	8.122
Papers of the U.S. Commission on Wartime Relocation and Internment of Civilians. [Reel index]	19.122
Papers relating to the foreign relations of the United States. Japan: 1931-1941	17.2
Papers relating to the massacre of Europeans at Tien-Tsin, 21st June, 1870	4.2
Papers respecting labour conditions in China	4.54
Paris Peace Conference, 1919. China	22.34
Paris peace talks on Vietnam, 1968-1973	34.18-34.182
Peking chronicle	10.32
People's Republic of China, 1949-1976: A documentary survey	10.38
Perry, Matthew Calbraith	22.1
Policy of the United States and Japan in the Far East	17.1
Political relations between China and other states, 1910-1929	8.14
Political relations of the United States with China, 1910-1929	8.16
Political reorientation of Japan, September 1945 to September 1948	20.22
PORTUGAL--COLONIES--MACAO	4.46
Postwar Japan, Korea, and Southeast Asia	21.18
Postwar Japan, Korea, and Southeast Asia. [Guide]	21.182
Preliminary inventory of the records of the War Relocation Authority	19.1

Prelude to infamy; official report on the final
    phase of U.S.-Japanese relations, October 17
    to December 7, 1941 .... 18.12
PRESBYTERIAN CHURCH--MISSIONS 10.11
Presbyterian Church in the USA. Board of Foreign
    Mission 10.11
Press translations and summaries. Japan 20.16
Prices and price indexes in Shanghai 2.24
PRICES--SHANGHAI 2.18, 2.24, 2.32
PRISONERS OF WAR--KOREA 32.1
PRISONS 9.1
Pritchard, R. John 20.11-20.112
Private collections, Jordan papers, 1910-1919 .... 4.35
Proclamations, statements and communications of
    the Manchoukuo government 23.1
Prussia. Armee. Grosser Generalstab. Kriegs-
    geschichtliche Abteilung 22.28
Publications of the Dept. of Foreign Affairs,
    Manchoukuo Government 23.16
Pusan perimeter 31.16
Quarterly journal of statistics [Nanking] 2.28
Quarterly returns of trade 1.14
Quist, Norm 18.102, 35.1
Rebec, Estelle 19.1
Recent progress in Korea 33.2
RECIPROCITY 21.12
RECONSTRUCTION--JAPAN 20.12
Records of the Department of State relating to [the]
    internal affairs of China, 1910-1929 .... 8.12-8.124
Records of the Department of State relating to
    internal affairs of Japan, 1910-1929 .... 17.14-17.142
Records of the Department of State relating to
    internal affairs of Japan [1930-1939 and
    1940-1944] 17.18
Records of the Department of State relating to
    political relations between China and other
    states, 1910-1929 .... 8.14
Records of the Department of State relating to
    political relations between Japan and other
    states, 1910-1929 .... 17.16
Records of the Department of State relating to
    political relations of the United States
    with China, 1910-1929 .... 8.16
Records of the Joint Chiefs of Staff: The Far
    East, 1946-53 .... 35.1
Records of the Joint Chiefs of Staff: The
    Pacific theater, 1942-1945 .... 18.19
Records of the Subcommittee for the Far East,
    1945-1948 .... 21.16
Records of the United States Consulate in Kunming,
    1922-28 .... 6.5
Records of the United State Legation in China,
    1843-1945 .... 6.14
Records of the U.S. Strategic Bombing Survey 18.2

Records of treaties, conventions, etc. between
   Manchoukuo and foreign states 23.22
Registers and indexes of general correspondence:
   China, 1815-1890 .... 4.102
Registers of general correspondence: China, Japan
   Siam, Korea, 1891-191 .... 4.104
Relations diplomatiques entre la Chine et la Japon
   de 1871 a nos jours [1921] 22.16
Relations of Japan with Manchuria and Mongolia 24.16
REPATRIATION--KOREA 32.18
Report by Mr. Baber on the route followed by Mr.
   Grosvenor's mission between Tali-fu and Momein ... 4.22
Report by Mr. C. W. Campbell, His Majesty's consul
   at Wuchow, on a journey in Mongolia 4.32
Report by Mr. Hosie on the Island of Formosa, with
   special reference to its resources and trade 3.14
Report of the advisory committee together with other
   documents respecting the China indemnity 4.56
Report of the Commission of Enquiry 26.18
Report of the Commission on Extraterritoriality in
   China, Peking, September 16, 1929 .... 9.1
Report on administration of Chosen 27.18
Report on current economy; Japan's economy under
   stabilization program 12.18
Report on economic and commercial conditions in
   China 5.12
Report on progress in Manchuria 24.1
Report on reforms and progress in Chosen (Korea) 27.18
Report on reforms and progress in Korea 27.18
Report on the commercial, industrial and economic
   situation of China 5.12
Report on the commercial, industrial, and
   financial situation in Japan 15.12
Report on the conditions and prospects of British
   trade with China 5.12
Report on the foreign trade 27.14
Report on the industrial and economic situation
   of China 5.12
Reports from Her Majesty's minister in China re-
   specting events at Peking...December 1900 .... 4.26
Reports from His Majesty's minister at Peking
   respecting the opium question in China 3.12
Reports of the U.S. Naval Technical Mission to
   Japan, 1945-1946 .... 20.26
Reports on the trade at the ports in China open by
   treaty to foreign trade 1.1
Reports on trade at the treaty ports 1.1
Reports on trade at the treaty ports in China 1.1
Reports to the League of Nations by the Committee
   of Representatives at Shanghai 22.42
Republic of Korea Army 27.24
Research aids on the People's Republic of China 7.12
Resume statistique de l'empire du Japon 13.12
Returns of trade and trade reports 1.11

Returns of trade at the treaty ports, and trade reports	1.118
Returns of trade at the treaty ports in China	1.118
Reynolds, Carol	4.182
Rockhill, William Woodville	33.14, 33.18
Rogin, Martin	19.1
Rozanski, Mordechai	8.124
RUSSIA--FOREIGN RELATIONS--CHINA	10.24, 25.12
RUSSIA--FOREIGN RELATIONS--JAPAN	11.12, 33.16
RUSSIA--FOREIGN RELATIONS--U.S.	30.12
Russia. Komissia po Opisaniiu Russko-iaponskoi Voiny 1904 i 1905 Godov	22.3-22.32
Russia. Treaties, etc.	33.24
Russia. Treaties, etc., 1894-1917 (Nicholas II)	11.12
RUSSIANS IN MANCHURIA	25.12
Russisch-japanische Krieg: Amtliche Darstellung des russischen Generalstabes	22.32
Russko-iaponskaia voina, 1904-1905 gg.	22.3
Russo-Japanese War	15.1, 22.28
RUSSO-JAPANESE WAR, 1904-1905	15.1, 22.26-22.32
Russo-Japanese War (official reports)	22.26
Saionji, Kinmochi	22.185
Saionji-Harada memoirs	22.185
Sakatani, Kiichi	24.24
Satow, Ernest Mason	33.16
SAVE OUR SONS COMMITTEE	32.16
Scherzer, Fernand	33.1
Schipper, Martin	8.302
Schlessinger, Kenneth D.	34.18-34.182
Scholarly Resources, Inc.	8.124, 14.102, 14.16-14.162, 14.202, 17.18-17.182, 18.195-18.197
Secret documents relating to the Japanese policy toward Manchuria and Mongolia	26.16
Select documents on Japanese foreign policy, 1853-1868	22.12
Service list	1.114
Sessional papers	5.14-5.16
Shanghai. Chinese General Chamber of Commerce	22.4
SHANGHAI--HISTORY	10.22
Shanghai market prices report	2.18
SHANGHAI--MARKETS	2.18, 2.24
Shantung question, a statement of China's claim together with important documents submitted to the Peace Conference in Paris	22.34
SHIPPING--CHINA	1.11, 1.12, 1.18
SHIPPING--KOREA	1.12
SINO-JAPANESE CONFLICT, 1937-1945	10.32-10.34
Sino-Japanese Conflict and the League of Nations, 1937	10.34
Sino-Japanese entanglements, 1931-1932 (a military record)	24.14

Sino-Japanese negotiations of 1915; Japanese and
    Chinese documents and Chinese official
    statement 22.36
Sino-Japanese War to the Russo-Japanese War,
    1894-1905 .... 10.2
South Korean Interim Government activities,
    United States Army Military Government
    in Korea 29.18
South Manchuria Railway Company 24.1, 24.26
Soviet Union and American intervention in
    Korea (documents) 30.12
Special report of the Unified Command on the Korean
    armistice agreement 30.34
Special series 1.119
Special studies of the International Military
    Tribunal for the Far East 22.58
Standard trade index of Japan 22.62
Statements of Japanese officials on World War II 18.24
Statistical abstract of Japan 13.22
Statistical handbook of Japan 13.24
Statistical monthly [Nanking] 2.28
Statistical survey of economy of Japan 12.28
Statistics of agriculture, industries and commerce .. 13.16
Statistics on Japanese industries 12.32
Subject and name index to the MAGIC documents 18.104
Summation, non-military activities in Japan 20.14
Summation, non-military activities in Japan and
    Korea 20.14
Summation, United States Army Military Government
    activities in Korea 29.18
Supreme Commander for the Allied Powers 20.14-20.16, 20.24
Supreme Commander for the Allied Powers. Economic
    and Scientific Section 12.14
Supreme Commander for the Allied Powers. Government
    Section 20.2-20.22, 22.56
Surrender documents in facsimile 18.22
Survey of economic conditions in Japan 22.38
TAIPING REBELLION, 1850-1864 .... 10.1
TAIWAN 3.14, 8.3-8.302, 10.36
Takenobu, Yoshitaro 22.24
Tanaka, Giichi, baron 26.16
TARIFF--CHINA 1.119
Temporary agreement supplementary to the
    Armistice agreement 30.32
Text of notes exchanged between the United States
    and Japanese governments regarding their
    policy in China 17.12
TEXTILE FACTORIES--CHINA 4.54
TIBET 4.3, 4.5
Toa-keizai Chosakyoku 24.12
Tokyo gazette 22.5
Tokyo war crimes trial 20.11
Tokyo war crimes trial. Index and guide 20.112
Trade of China 1.24

TRADE REGULATION--CHINA--SHANGHAI	4.24
Trade statistics of the treaty ports, for the period 1863-1872	1.26
Traites et conventions entre l'Empire du Japon et les puissances etrangeres	11.14
Transcripts and files of the Paris peace talks on Vietnam, 1968-1973	34.18-34.182
Translation of official report concerning the attack on the Royal Palace at Seoul, Korea	27.16
Treaties and conventions with or concerning China and Korea, 1894-1904	33.14
Treaties between the United States of America and China, Japan, Lewchew and Siam	21.1
Treaties, conventions, etc. between China and foreign states	1.28
Treaties, regulations, etc. between Corea and other powers, 1876-1889	27.1
Treatment of British prisoners of war in Korea	32.14
Treaty and protocol between the United States and Japan. Commerce and navigation	21.12
Treaty system and the Taiping Rebellion, 1842-1860	10.1
Trial of Japan war criminals. Documents	20.1
Union Research Institute	10.42
United Nations action in Korea under unified command	31.12
United Nations Command	30.26, 30.32-30.34, 31.2
United Nations Command. Military Armistice Commission	30.32
UNITED NATIONS--KOREA	29.12, 31.12
United Nations. Security Council	30.12
United States [author]	31.12
United States agreements with the Republic of Korea	28.18
United States and the Korean problem: Documents, 1943-1953	29.1
U.S. armed forces in Vietnam, 1954-1975	34.12
U.S.--ARMED FORCES--VIETNAM	34.12-34.122
U.S. Army. Civil Affairs Division	20.18, 20.24
U.S. Army. Far East Command	22.185
U.S. Army. Forces in Korea	29.18, 31.1
U.S. Army. Forces in the Far East	29.18, 32.12, 32.18
U.S. Army. Forces in the Pacific	29.18
United States Army in the Korean Conflict	31.14
U.S. Army. Manhattan Engineer District	18.23-18.232
United States Army Military Government in Korea	29.18
U.S. Army. Office of Military History	31.14
U.S. Army. Pacific Division. Offfice of the Assistant Chief of Staff, G-3. Military History Office	32.1
U.S. ARMY--SUPPLIES AND STORES	32.12
U.S. Board of Economic Warfare	18.18
U.S. Central Intelligence Agency	7.1-7.12, 21.2, 34.1-34.102

United States, China, and imperial rivalries	10.16
United States-China relations, 1940-1949	8.215-8.2152
U.S.--COMMERCE--CHINA	9.12
U.S.--COMMERCE--JAPAN	21.12
U.S. Commission on Wartime Relocation and Internment of Civilians	19.1-19.122
U.S. Congress. House. Committee on Un-American Activities	32.16
U.S. Congress. Senate. Committee on Armed Services	30.14-30.18
U.S. Congress. Senate. Committee on Foreign Relations	29.1, 30.14, 30.18
U.S. Consulate, Amoy, China	6.18
U.S. Consulate, Antung, China	6.46
U.S. Consulate, Canton, China	6.1
U.S. Consulate, Chefoo, China	6.34
U.S. Consulate, Chingkiang, China	6.36
U.S. Consulate, Chungking, China	6.4
U.S. Consulate, Foochow, China	6.24
U.S. Consulate General, Yokohama, Japan	16.22
U.S. Consulate, Hakodate, Japan	16.16
U.S. Consulate, Hangchow, China	6.48
U.S. Consulate, Hankow, China	6.32
U.S. Consulate, Hong Kong	6.2
U.S. Consulate, Kobe, Japan	16.2
U.S. Consulate, Kunming, China	6.5
U.S. Consulate, Macao	6.26
U.S. Consulate, Mukden, Manchuria	25.14
U.S. Consulate, Nagasaki, Japan	16.18
U.S. Consulate, Nanking, China	6.44
U.S. Consulate, Newchang, China	25.1
U.S. Consulate, Ningpo, China	6.28
U.S. Consulate, Seoul, Korea	28.16
U.S. Consulate, Shanghai, China	6.22
U.S. Consulate, Swatow, China	6.3
U.S. Consulate, Tan-shui, Formosa	6.42
U.S. Consulate, Tientsin, China	6.38
U.S. Dept. of State	2.1, 6.1-6.5, 8.1-8.26, 8.28-8.282, 9.14, 9.145, 11.1, 16.1-17.24, 17.26, 18.12, 20.1-20.12, 21.14, 21.18-21.182, 27.12, 28.1-28.16
U.S. Dept. of State. Office of Northeast Asian Affairs	17.24
U.S. Dept. of State. Office of Public Affairs	29.12
U.S. Embassy. Korea	28.18
U.S. Far East Command. Military Intelligence Section. Historical Division	18.24
U.S.--FOREIGN POLICY--CHINA	8.215-8.2152
U.S.--FOREIGN RELATIONS--20TH CENTURY	17.16
U.S.--FOREIGN RELATIONS--ASIA	21.2

U.S.--FOREIGN RELATIONS--CHINA	6.12, 8.1, 8.22-8.26, 9.115, 9.12, 10.12-10.14, 10.28, 17.12, 25.1, 25.14
U.S.--FOREIGN RELATIONS--CHINA--SOURCES	8.215-8.2152, 9.11, 10.1, 10.16, 10.2
U.S.--FOREIGN RELATIONS--EAST ASIA	35.1
U.S.--FOREIGN RELATIONS--JAPAN	8.22, 11.1, 16.1-17.12, 17.16, 17.2, 17.24, 18.12, 21.14
U.S.--FOREIGN RELATIONS--KOREA	27.12, 28.1-29.1, 30.1, 33.12-33.13
U.S.--FOREIGN RELATIONS--MANCHURIA	25.1, 25.14
U.S.--FOREIGN RELATIONS--RUSSIA	30.12
U.S.--FOREIGN RELATIONS--TREATIES	21.1
U.S. International Trade Administration	9.12
U.S. Joint Chiefs of Staff	18.19, 35.1
U.S. Joint Intelligence Center, Pacific Ocean Areas	18.2
U.S. Legation (China)	6.14
U.S. Marine Corps	31.16
U.S. Marine operations in Korea, 1950-1953	31.16
U.S. military intelligence reports: China, 1911-1941	9.11
U.S.--MILITARY RELATIONS--EAST ASIA	21.16
U.S. National Archives [and Records Service]	6.1-6.5, 8.16, 8.124, 8.2-8.202, 8.21-8.212, 8.215-8.2152, 8.28-8.282, 11.1, 16.1-17.24, 18.14, 18.2-18.22, 19.1, 21.16, 25.1, 25.14, 27.12, 28.1-28.16
U.S. National Security Council	34.16-34.162
U.S. NAVAL EXPEDITION TO JAPAN, 1852-1854	10.14, 22.1
U.S. Naval Historical Center. Operational Archives	18.195-18.197
U.S. Naval Technical Mission to Japan	20.26
U.S. Navy. Joint Intelligence Center, Pacific Ocean Areas	18.195-18.197
U.S. Navy. Pacific Fleet and Pacific Ocean Areas	18.195-18.197
U.S. Office of Naval Intelligence	18.2
U.S. Office of Strategic Services	9.14, 9.145, 18.16-18.162, 21.18-21.182
United States policy toward China: Diplomatic and public documents, 1839-1939	10.12
United States relations with China, with special reference to the period 1944-1949	8.26
United States relations with Japan, 1945-1952	17.24
U.S. State-War-Navy Coordinating Committee. Subcommittee for the Far East	21.16
U.S. Strategic Bombing Survey	18.2
U.S. Treaties, etc.	21.1, 21.14, 33.14, 33.18
U.S. Treaties, etc., 1909-1913 (Taft)	21.12

U.S. War Dept.	9.11, 18.1, 19.14, 20.18, 20.24
U.S. War Relocation Authority	19.1-19.122
University Publications of America	8.2, 8.202, 8.21-8.212, 8.215-8.2152, 8.28-8.282, 8.3-8.302, 9.11, 9.115, 9.145, 10.44, 16.24, 17.23-17.232, 17.26, 18.1-18.104, 18.16-18.162, 18.19, 18.23-18.232, 19.12-19.122, 21.18-21.182, 21.2, 21.22-21.222, 34.1-35.122
Verdict of the League; China and Japan in Manchuria	26.2
Vietnam: A documentary collection	34.13
Vietnam and Southeast Asia, 1946-1976	34.1-34.102
Vietnam and Southeast Asia: Special studies, 1960-1980	34.14
VIETNAM--BIBLIOGRAPHY	34.142
VIETNAM--HISTORY--1946-1980	34.1-34.102, 34.14-34.142
Vietnam: National Security Council histories	34.16-34.162
VIETNAMESE CONFLICT, 1961-1975	34.12-34.122, 34.16-34.182
WAR CRIMES TRIALS--TOKYO, 1946-1948	20.1-20.112, 22.58
War in Vietnam	34.16-34.162
Watt, Donald Cameron	20.11
Weekly report on Japan	20.24
Westmoreland, William Childs	34.13
Westmoreland v. CBS	34.13
WEI-HAI-WEI, CHINA	4.44
White papers of Japan	12.36
Who's who in Manchuria	24.12
Wilbur, Clarence Martin	10.24
Williams, Samuel Wells	10.14
WORLD WAR, 1939-1945--DIPLOMATIC HISTORY	18.1
WORLD WAR, 1939-1945--EAST ASIA	18.19-18.2
WORLD WAR, 1939-1945--EVACUATION OF CIVILIANS--BIBLIOGRAPHY	19.1
WORLD WAR, 1939-1945--GREAT BRITAIN--SOURCES	14.16-14.162, 14.2-14.202
WORLD WAR, 1939-1945--JAPAN	11.22, 14.16-14.162, 14.2-14.202, 18.1-18.104, 18.2-18.24, 20.26
WORLD WAR, 1939-1945--LAW AND LEGISLATION--INDONESIA	22.54
WORLD WAR, 1939-1945--MILITARY INTELLIGENCE--PACIFIC OCEAN	18.195-18.197
WORLD WAR, 1939-1945--MILITARY OPERATIONS, AMERICAN--SOURCES	18.195-18.2
WORLD WAR, 1939-1945--OCCUPIED TERRITORIES	22.54
WORLD WAR, 1939-1945--OCEANIA	18.19
WORLD WAR, 1939-1945--PACIFIC OCEAN	11.18, 18.19-18.2
WORLD WAR, 1939-1945--PEACE PROPOSALS AND SETTLEMENTS	11.22, 18.22

WORLD WAR, 1939-1945--SECRET SERVICE--U.S.	18.195-18.197
WORLD WAR, 1939-1945--U.S.	18.14
Yang, Kuang-sheng	10.34
Yingling, J. M.	31.16
Yunesuko Higashi Ajia Bunka Kenkyu Senta, Tokyo	22.14
Zaide, Sonia M.	20.11-20.112

RAYMOND H. FOGLER LIBRARY
DATE DUE

BOOKS ARE SUBJECT TO
RECALL AFTER TWO WEEKS